A Letter To My Abuser:
Once a Victim, Forever Victorious

Sharisa T. Robertson

www.lotfmedia.com

A Letter To My Abuser: Once a Victim, Forever Victorious

ISBN: 978-0-9854961-4-2

Published by Lilies of the Field Media, LLC, Detroit, MI info@lotfmedia.com

Cover Design: Alegna Media www.alegnamediasuite.com
Editing: Tamykah Anthony-Marston
Book Layout: Usama Waqur

Lilies of the Field Media, LLC and its authors hope that you will find encouragement, inspiration, and information within the pages of this book.

Happy Reading and Welcome to our world!!!!

Presented To:

Reach for the Victory!
Peace, Love, Joy,

From:

Turelise Smith

Date:

2020

Dedication

Whether you're wallowing in your fear or standing in your power
Whether you're ready to face your truth or hide behind the secrets
and lies
Whether you're currently being abused or was once a victim
Whether you've been silent or vocal about your experience

No matter if you've forgiven your abuser or can't fathom the
thought of forgiveness right now
No matter your emotional or mental state
No matter your coping mechanism or self-care rituals
No matter if you're living in the past, struggling in the present or
daydreaming for a better future

This book is dedicated to you, was written for you, regardless of
where you are or what you've experience in your journey.

May one thing resonate in your soul to pivot you into your best
you.

Table of Contents

Foreword

Sharisa Robertson has curated this collection of letters from survivors of domestic and sexual violence, who have poured out their raw emotions and have given us a glimpse into their experiences of abuse.

I founded the nonprofit organization, **Sisters Acquiring Financial Empowerment (SAFE)**, in April 2006 to help survivors of domestic violence overcome the economic effects of abuse. I am a survivor of domestic and sexual violence, a national domestic violence trainer and a keynote speaker. I have consistently stressed the importance of victims being given a voice and for our stories to be heard and believed.

I hope you will open your mind and your heart when reading the heartfelt letters featured in this book, *A Letter To My Abuser*. I also hope that these letters spark a new movement of compassion towards victims of domestic and sexual violence. Please join us in our mission to support victims and stop the blaming of victims for the abuse that was inflicted upon them. Honoring and listening to survivors of domestic and sexual violence is important to healing not only the survivors, but ending domestic violence, healing our homes and our communities on a global scale.

Be encouraged.

Kalyn Risker Fahle

Sisters Acquiring Financial Empowerment (SAFE)
www.newsafestart.org

1

Preface

"I am going to do a book project for women who have been abused, *A Letter To My Abuser*." This was my thought while I was in the process of publishing my first book collaboration, *A Letter To My Mother: A Daughter's Perspective*, for women who have struggled and continue to struggle in strained relationships with their mothers. Then, after publishing my second collaboration, *A Letter To My Bully: Sticks, Stones, and Words Do Hurt*, for young girls who've been bullied, I decided it was time to do it. Now, almost 5 years later, what was once a thought is now an actual book that you have in your hands.

Delayed but not denied right?

Although I am not a confrontational person by nature, I make it my mission to use this book and my other projects as tools to confront issues that people may find too hurtful to discuss. I am always doubtful, hesitant, and unsure if anyone will share such personal, traumatic, and often taboo stories with me. Then, as I am going through the publishing process, I wonder whether anyone will even want to read the stories.

I thank God I was able to make this project come to life because I realize now that this book is needed. It was hard and there were many obstacles. These obstacles led to missed deadlines and, as things were not going according to my vision, I found myself feeling discouraged in the middle of doing the project. I pushed through though, and the women who shared their stories pushed themselves even harder and, in the end, the outcome far exceeded my original vision.

2

Every time you turn a page in this book you bear witness to the epitome of resilience. The book was a work of labor for us all, but to actually experience what you will soon read and still be here to tell it, is a true testament in itself.

Yes, abuse against women unfortunately isn't anything new and this is not the first book that deals with and talks about abuse. *A Letter To My Abuser* takes a unique approach to addressing abuse because women need to be provided a platform to release. They are expected to get over it, to not feel, damn sure not be scared, angry or have an attitude, but yet carry the shame and blame of the abuse while embodying this warped definition of being strong women, mothers, wives, etc.

Where can abused women go to freely talk about abuse?

Who can they talk to?

Where are their support systems?

To be abused is to be improperly handled and thankfully these women don't look like what they have been through, but make no mistake, lives are definitely altered when women are mistreated.

Lives are altered when women are not allowed to be vulnerable. Lives are altered when women have to carry the weight of being abused. It becomes not just something that happened to you but a part of you and every decision you make.

The first part of the journey is surviving the abuse while it is happening, the next is leaving the abuse whether it be a mental, an emotional, a spiritual decision, or a physical departure, and the final part is learning how to live after the abuse.

3

This book allows these brave women to unearth the raw emotional truth buried deep in their painful stories of abuse. And they went in, in their own unique way, with their own unique voice and experience.

My vision.
Their stories.
Our book.
Your empowerment.

Sharisa T. Robertson

Introduction

They say a bullet has no name. Well, neither does abuse. It pierces through the soul of any and all with no regard, leaving a wound in the abused, and the one pulling the trigger, especially in the case of these authors, is a loved one. Since hurt people can hurt people, I wonder what happened to the abusers that would make them commit these acts of violence against the women/young girls in their lives.

The statistics regarding abuse against women are alarming enough. But, when coupled with the fact that abuse usually goes unreported, ignored, or undetected, those numbers go from alarming to unacceptable. Women face abuse in many different ways. It can be from a loved one, a stranger, an associate, self-inflicted, systematic or situational.

Abuse is a noun and a verb, an act and an action. Abuse is a behavior that is manifested through people, systems, and situations and is a construct within itself making up a larger system of abuse. It is the misuse of someone or something, to be cruel or violent, especially regularly or repeatedly. It is a false sense of control over someone. It is intentional and unintentional harm to another.

Whether verbal, emotional, mental, physical, sexual, financial, social, psychological, economic, spiritual, parental, familial, workplace, bullying, harassment or neglect, abuse takes on all these forms. Although all of these are not addressed in this book, it is important to point out that abuse is not limited in its ways.

This book embodies the voice, the resilience, and the raw truth about abuse by getting deep into the wounds of those who have experienced it firsthand.

Imagine being able to talk to the person who abused you, hurt you, or mistreated you. No holds barred and no interruptions.

What would you say?

What would you hold them accountable for? Yourself?

What hurt from their abuse would you share with them?

What scars would you show? What wounds would you let them see?

How deep would you go?

Would you even bother?

Maybe you don't know the answers. Maybe you do. What are the chances that you will be given the opportunity to confront your abuser and talk about the impact it had on you?

It is slim to none.

With *A Letter To My Abuser*, we are not waiting for a chance to be given. I created a platform for these seven women (and myself) to stand on and share our truth unapologetically. When I read their letters for the first time, my mind was blown and my heart opened. When I wrote my letter, my spirit sighed with relief.

The hearts of women cannot be contained. Neither can their rage or their words as they heal. Read the letters. Be educated, enlightened and empowered by the resources shared.

A Letter To My Abuser: Once a Victim, Forever Victorious is filled with letters (of course). After each letter, the authors write words of encouragement to you, the reader, to help you reclaim or even remember your victory in the Words of Wisdom and Love section. Be guided by their advice.

The second half of the book is additional information about abuse along with a directory of places to contact for support.

Lastly, there is a bonus section. Here, you can write a letter to YOUR abuser, making you an unofficial author of this book as well, but, more importantly, an official author of your life and your healing. There is power in the pen, please believe it.

The purpose of this book is the following:

- To provide an outlet for those who have been abused
- To raise awareness about the different forms of abuse
- To be the voice and advocate for the abused
- To shift the narrative of the abused from victim to victorious
- To allow these women an authentic, safe and uncensored space to express their thoughts and experiences.
- To provide a space and an opportunity to heal
- To use writing as the therapeutic tool that it is
- To turn pain into purpose
- To talk about what to do after abuse.

This book is therapeutic. It is awareness. It is painful. It is freedom. It is for those who have risen from the ashes to find their beauty in something so ugly.

This collaboration is necessary because our voices need to be heard and our stories told. And it is even more necessary that our scars (inside and out) be healed in order to end the destructive cycle of abuse.

Powerful stories. Even more powerful women.

I welcome you to *A Letter To My Abuser: Once a Victim, Forever Victorious.*

Sharisa T. Robertson

Journey Within

Furelise Smith

Dear Spirit of My Brother, My Childhood Protector, My Childhood Confidante, My Childhood Abuser,

*W*ho would I be had you not raped me? I choose to communicate with your spirit because I know there is no time or space in spirit. Spirit is unlimited. Also, I know our spirits hold the key to my continued growth and healing. And..there is no "body" for me to speak with....for you are now totally in the Spirit realm, which actually makes writing this letter so much easier. I am not dealing with your humanness—ego, mental or emotional beingness. No need for me to censor myself.

The insidious thing about having been raped by you as a child, is that here I am over half a century later still reeling from that experience. I never know what is going to trigger a memory. Recently, I was triggered by the idea of having to sleep in a room with bunk beds while on vacation. Bunk beds? Really?? Yes, REALLY!!

The memories are stored in my body, my mind and my emotions. You...a bold eleven year old boy. Me...an obedient eight year old girl. You loved, protected and cared for me. I adored, admired and would do anything you asked. I was your little sister. You were my older brother. I was readily available. We shared a room with bunk beds. (TRIGGER!) You easily manipulated me. I followed your directions: "Come down to my bunk. Open your legs. Let me put IT in."

In the moments that I was being raped by you, my mind was filled with various incongruent thoughts and my body was filled with various unfamiliar emotions. "This is wrong. My brother loves and protects me, I can't tell him

'No!' If our parents find out, we're in serious trouble. My body feels really good. This has to be kept a secret!"

Now, years later, my mind always goes back and forth when making decisions...seldom straight to: "What do YOU want, Furelise?" My emotions often elude me: "What is it I am feeling???" Continually feeling obligated, responsible, keeping secrets and searching for answers, makes me weary. In my head is where I was while you raped me. Now, decades later, still in my head, the problem is....once inside my head, I have to decide which one of the residents I'm going to listen to. Who can best be of service today in this particular situation?

- THE WOUNDED, CONFUSED LITTLE GIRL who is still trying to make some sense of herself and her experiences.... usually her solution is to throw some sort of tantrum. I've named her Boomsheika; she has a tendency to go 'Boom.'

- THE COMPLIANT, OBEDIENT ADOLESCENT who never considered doing anything to upset anyone, particularly those she perceived to be in authority... parents, teachers, adults, a Brother.

DISOBEDIENCE WAS NOT AN OPTION.

- THE YOUNG, YOUNG ADULT at college, away from home, being mildly rebellious, who was totally unaware of the connection between her childhood experiences of sexual violation and her anger.

- THE OLDER YOUNG ADULT who, when experiencing the pleasurable physical sensations of an intimate sexual experience with a man, had the feelings in her body, then the thoughts in her mind: "This is how it felt when I was a child and my brother

11

raped   me. Oh shit! What the hell??"

- THE COURAGEOUS YOUNG ADULT who prior to going to visit her brother and his family, wrote him a letter describing what she remembered about the experience of childhood sexual violation and asked if he shared that memory. He never replied. So while visiting she inquired:

  Me: "Did you get my letter?"

  You: "Yes."

  Me: "Well?"

  You: "I don't remember anything specific, but it doesn't sound like something that DIDN'T happen."

  Me: (interpretation of your response) That's as close as I'm going to get to a "Yes, it did happen" from him----A NON-DENIAL. You're on your own with this one Furelise, he cannot help you. You, my dear brother, chose to abandon me when I needed you most.

- THE EMOTIONALLY MATURE ADULT who now knows that when she wrote that letter she was unable to ask you directly if you remembered sexually abusing her. Instead she insinuated that you did, and she was hoping for your validation and an apology. She thought your admission would alleviate the guilt and shame she felt. She thought an apology would soothe her and make her feel better. NOT! Her desire for an apology was based on the supposition that you too, felt ashamed and guilty. She now knows that shame and guilt were HER emotions and may never have been considered and/or felt by you.

12

- THE SEXUALLY ACTIVE ADULT who was too often in relationships being loyal and monogamous with men she did not trust; too often letting herself be chosen rather than making a conscious decision to be with a particular man; too often staying in relationships when she was being misused and/or abused; too often unwilling to open herself up in a relationship for fear of being misused and/or abused; too often not knowing how to be in a relationship and take care of herself at the same time.

TOO OFTEN...

The ramifications of being sexually violated by you as a child have been evident in all aspects of my life—physical, emotional, spiritual and of course sexual. My relationship with my body—physical pleasuring of myself—was initially taboo and then became a task, a goal to accomplish, a way to take back my power from the memory of complying with your direction to open my legs so you could put IT, your penis, in my vagina.

My experience of being raped by you, my brother, taught me some valuable life lessons. I've learned to be empathetic towards others because I know that people have experiences that can change the trajectory of their lives without their understanding, knowledge and/or consent.

When I observe 'misbehaving' adults, I wonder what childhood experiences contributed to their present day actions. What are their triggers? Do they even know when they're being triggered? Do they understand why they're being triggered? I've learned that keeping secrets can kill you—your spirit, your access to your emotions and quite possibly your body. Because I couldn't tell anyone about the sexual violation, I spent a lot of my life not knowing what my feelings were and/or why I felt a certain way.

Feeling anger totally eluded me: "I don't get angry!" Meanwhile, I'm cussing folks out...often only in MY head, occasionally out loud....and then being angry with myself for being angry! I turned the anger inward...DEPRESSION. Where else could I put the anger other than on myself? Why didn't I take better care of myself? Why didn't I tell you, my brother, "NO!"? Why did we have parents who were unaware of what was going on in the bedroom next to theirs? What thoughts were you, my eleven year old brother, thinking when you sexually violated me?

Why was I misbehaving and being wrong? Of course, unconsciously, I decided that I couldn't be wrong about anything else in my life. So, I lived my life trying to be perfect, keeping things in order, UNDER CONTROL, so that wrong couldn't enter into my psyche or experiences anywhere. I MUST DO THE RIGHT THING, NO MATTER WHAT! The need to do the right thing and to be right while doing it wreaked havoc with my sense of personal well-being. This havoc led to anger, which led to depression which led to suicidal thoughts:

> Do I really have any value/worth? Why am I even here on earth? Maybe I shouldn't be here on earth? Perhaps I can do something about NOT being here on earth?

Fortunately, for me, the spirit within me used that last thought to scare me into seeking help. My willingness to seek help and my ability to find competent, professional healthcare practitioners, who provided guidance and support, and most importantly, my dedication and commitment to continued growth and healing, has saved me from myself.

14

I learned this mantra:

> I AM NOT TO BLAME.
>
> I DID NOTHING WRONG.
>
> I AM A SURVIVOR.

It's not about surviving being sexually abused. It's about surviving the things I told myself, about myself, because I was sexually abused. HARD, HEALING WORK. [Of which writing this letter is a part of.]

Dear Thoughts I Told Myself About Myself Because I Was Raped By My Brother,

I FORGIVE YOU.

Peace and Love,

Once a Victim, Now Victorious Me,

Furelise

Words of Wisdom and Love

ALL things ALWAYS work together for good,
in ALL WAYS.....ALWAYS.
IT'S UP TO ME TO SEE THE WAYS.

AUTHOR'S BIO

Furelise Barbara Smith was born and raised in New York City. She earned her
Undergraduate & Master's Degrees from State University of New York
Colleges near
Rochester, New York. There she served as an
Educator in the Rochester City School District for 32 years.
Living and loving her life as a 'free-tired'
Individual, she spends the winter months in the
Southern states of Georgia and Florida
Enjoying quality time with family and friends.

Being a wordsmith has
Always been her passion.
Revealing and sharing who she is
Becomes easy–flows–whenever she puts pen to paper.
Awarenessses that she may have difficulty verbalizing
Re-present as prose or poetry, seamlessly, when she writes. Thus
Actualizing

Spirit's
Manifestations
In, as, around and
Through her,
Here and now.

You Broke Me,

"But" You Didn't Destroy Me,

Love's Got Everything to Do

With It

Cathy Staton

Dear Abuser,

The day I met you, the warning stared me in my face and I never saw it. After our very rude and uncomfortable first encounter, I should have never answered your call. As soon as I realized it was you, I should have said no and hung up. But you could see right through me couldn't you? You saw things in me that I didn't even see in myself. How did you know I was broken, stripped of my dignity and looking for love? How did you know that my self-esteem was all the way to the ground? Did I look desperate, or weak? What was it about me?

During our long talks I told you stories about how other men had treated me and put their hands on me and that I didn't want to be beat on anymore. I told you I didn't want to be cut anymore, hurt anymore. Yet you still hurt me, beat me, called me names, belittled me, you took away every last bit of self-worth that I had left. Why?

You were supposed to love me, honor me, protect me, and be there for me. But instead, loving you came with a price. You were good at hiding who you truly were. Congratulations, the award goes to you. You were good at convincing me that you truly loved me and the whole time you never knew what love was.

The funny thing is neither did I. I was lead to believe that love meant abuse. Not just from you but from my childhood, and past relationships. Somehow I thought you were going to save me from all the hurt and pain that I had been through, but all you did was make it worse.

For years I made myself feel like nothing just to make you feel like everything and it wasn't good enough. You had to control me and treat me like someone who could not do anything on their own. You wanted me to need you for everything. I was too broken to realize I was my own woman. You made me think I could not believe in myself.

It took only six months for you to show your true character. The whole time we dated all the way up into our marriage not one time did I see how narcissistic you were behind your lying eyes. The more I fell out of love with you, the more aggressive and angrier you became. Every day my son and I felt like we were walking on eggshells. We never knew if you were going to be Dr. Jekyll or Mr. Hyde. We couldn't do anything right in your eyes. Why did you marry me?

You did the same thing to your ex-wife. What happened in your childhood to make you so angry with women? What happened to turn you into a monster when someone tells you no? The first time you choked me I thought "not again!" Then I would beat myself up trying to figure out what I did to make you so angry and want to put your hands on me. Didn't you know I was already carrying around hurt and pain and you put more hurt and pain on top of more hurt and pain until I became trapped in a world where I couldn't see.

Your words broke me into tiny pieces and the more you verbally abused me the smaller I broke. The head butts and the broken hand reduced me to so much shame. Three times I almost lost my life with you. Why would you try and kill us? Did you hate us that much? Do you realize that my stomach is messed up today from the poisons you put in my food?

I cannot understand why you tried to hurt me so much. You wanted to inflict pain in me even when it was supposed to be pleasure. I paid highly for your sexual addiction. No matter how much I tried, I could never compete with women who do porn. Sex between a married man and women is supposed to be beautiful. You made it a night mare. I cannot count how many times you sexually assaulted me. You didn't care whether I wanted it or not. You were always in control and if I didn't do what you wanted, my days were going to be a living hell. You fed on my insecurities and you thought you had hit the jackpot.

Your sarcastic remarks, your condescending tone; your behavior took the life out of my body. I walked around spaced out like a zombie. I was your victim. You tried to destroy me. You were a retired drill sergeant and I was your cadet. I allowed you to use and manipulate me. I was too afraid to face what was happening to me. I trusted you and believed that you loved me. But how could you love me when you didn't know how to love yourself. I never thought I would be able to get away from you.

I want you to know that you are powerless. The only time you have power is when you get a victim and I pray that no other person has to go through what I went through with you. You depend on a victim's weakness to paint a false image of yourself and that is sickening. Your world is shattered and harming others brings you pleasure.

I thank God for sending for me again. This time I answered. Learning about God and His Word was life changing for me. I want to thank you for that. Had I not met you, I probably would have never met God. I want you to know that I forgive you. You see, in order for God to use me the way that He wanted to, I had to forgive you and all of those involved in our situation. Once I forgave, my transformation began. God showed me what love is and how to love myself. He showed me that love does not hurt.

Deciding to leave you for the third and final time was life changing for me. I discovered that I was bruised, but not broken. I discovered that God was going to give me beauty for my ashes. I learned from God that I was not all the names you called me. I learned that you have no clue what love is and that you hate yourself. Every single thing that you stripped me of, I got back better. You no longer have control over me. I have a new life and there is no turning back.

I want to thank you for helping me walk and live in my God-given purpose. I ran to God and He showed me a way out. Thank you for showing me how strong I was and helping me to see all the potential that I have inside of me. You knocked me down but I am standing tall like a giant. It is a beautiful thing to be free and to learn how to love myself inside and out. I know my worth. You can't hurt me anymore. I don't have to be afraid of you anymore.

I pray for you daily to get the help you need because you are a time bomb ticking and looking for your next victim. You have everyone fooled, but they don't know who you are behind closed doors. Love is beautiful, love feels good. They say love is blind, I say that it is not. It is we that are blind because we refuse to see or believe that the person we love is hurting us.

Love comes from God and within. I pray you learn to love yourself. Marriages and relationships should be valued and cherished. Thank you for putting a fight in me that will help many. I fight for those that are still out there in the hands of abusers like you. I fight for those who don't have a voice and are afraid to speak just like I was. I fight for those who've lost their lives to abuse because it could have been me.

But I thank God for saving me. I just want you to know that Love's got everything to do with it.

You are forgiven, God showed me how to receive and give love.

Because of you, I Own My Worth, Self-Esteem, and Value,

Author Cathy Staton

Words of Wisdom and Love

God is love.
God did not design us to hurt one another.
Love yourself more, know and own your worth, set yourself
free, love does not hurt.

AUTHOR'S BIO

Cathy Staton brings with her over 20 years of leadership development experience. Cathy is an author, motivational speaker, philanthropist, and life coach. Cathy Staton has become a trailblazer with a reputation for tenaciously helping women heal and walk in their purpose. Managing a successful nonprofit and teaching cutting edge life skill strategies join uncompromising integrity as the hallmark of Cathy's service. Fortunately, as an author and speaker, Cathy has a passion to tell her story and share the tools she used to not only survive, but thrive. Cathy is respected and well known in Hampton Roads, not only for her philanthropy work, but for doing absolutely everything in her power to ensure her clients' success. A self-published author and more importantly a "survivor" who provides messages of hope, inspiration, humor and encourage people to find their voice and use life's stumbling blocks to rebuild their own lives. She is the CEO and founder of **MyHelpMyHope Foundation, Inc.**, a 501c3 nonprofit organization that assists women and children in crisis situations. She is the CEO of **Dorcas, LLC.** Specifically, **Dorcas, LLC.**, provides affordable life-coaching to those who want to reach their maximum potential. Through one-on-one coaching, group coaching and custom presentations, she uses proven techniques to help people find fulfillment in their lives while doing what they love. Cathy is the recipient of the Wavy TV Channel 10 Who Care Award, the ZETA Phi Beta Sorority, Inc. Finer Woman Award, Hampton Roads Gazeti Exemplar Award, ACHI Magazine Woman of the year Award, and the Garden of Hope Unity Award from Gethsemane Community Fellowship Church, among others. Cathy's organizations' work has been featured on many television stations such as Tribune Media and Media General. Cathy has also been featured in publications such as the Virginia Pilot, and the New Journal and Guide, the Gazeti, and Tidewater Women, to name a few.

Dysfunction Comes in Many Different Faces

Christina A. Jiles

Dear Dysfunction,

ife was great until you showed up. I guess you were always lurking in the background but, before the age of 10, I knew nothing about you. Sure, our family life was a bit strained but we made it work the best we could. I didn't realize what you were until Daddy got sick with cancer. Daddy had been previously married and had several children prior to him marrying Mama. He was seventeen years her senior so there was this huge age difference that affected his children from his previous marriage too I'm sure.

Anyway, growing up I longed for the family vacations and holiday dinners but they never happened. The dynamics of a family like mine can be pretty weird when your siblings are old enough to be your parents and your parents are old enough to be your grandparents. We weren't as close as we could have been thanks to you, Dysfunction.

My Mama and siblings had issues years before I was born and I do mean YEARS! You made me hate you and everything you EVER stood for which is to divide, dissuade and devour if given the chance.

As Daddy's sickness progressed, so did the arguments. You really had your chest stuck out around that time Dysfunction. I remember it was because of you that my sister and Mama argued relentlessly while my Daddy laid on the couch helpless and crying. I tried to make them shut up but no one heard me. They were way too wrapped up in you....being dysfunctional. So wrapped up that they couldn't hear the cries and couldn't feel the pain. Can't feel anything but anger when you're in the room...let me tell ya!

Daddy fought for as long as he could against his lung

cancer but he died from complications. That was the hardest thing to ever live through because I was closest to him. We did everything together. Even my Mama and I's relationship was strained. She worked most of the time so Daddy took care of me while she was working. We'd do all kinds of things together and I loved every minute of it. He was my absolute best friend and then...he was gone. At the age of 10, I had to say goodbye to my best friend. I felt so lonely and Dysfunction, even then you still couldn't leave us alone. More arguing, more bickering, more flared tempers and now I was alone in it.

Who could I turn to? Daddy was gone, Mama was upset and everybody who came around before just stopped coming. They didn't care...did they? I was so confused and hurt. It only took me a little while to realize that this was only the beginning. Dysfunction, you were here to stay.

I wasn't the kid allowed to ride their bikes all over the neighborhood or even have a lot of friends. I led a very sheltered life. I guess in a sense now I was all my Mama had so she was very overprotective. Thankfully, there was a family in my neighborhood that served as my "second family."

I'd go with them to Church and attend their family dinners. Other than that, I'd only see that sort of thing on TV. I really looked at them as grandparents and their kids as aunts or cousins in a sense. We had so much fun. I was with them the first time I'd ever gotten into a pool and all that fun stuff that children love to do at that age. They had been friends with my Daddy so they helped Mama with me and took me to school and stuff like that too. I was at my happiest with them most of the times because it got me away from you, Dysfunction. I could go and laugh and have fun without having to worry about when you'd show up. At least that's what I thought.

One Sunday I chose not to go to Church with my other family. I was going to sit this one out but I went and visited with them and ate breakfast with them before they left. While everyone was getting dressed the man of the house who I'll call "Terry" decided to ask me something that I knew was very inappropriate.

After Daddy died "Terry" became a lot more touchy-feely. He'd hug me a lot and tell me he loved me and I was like, "ok, I get it...this is what Grandpas do!" Nevermind, I didn't have a strong relationship with my grandparents. They were a lot older and my paternal Grandmother barely spoke English so then there was that! Anyway, I didn't really think of it as anything bad at first but it became more frequent. Then I'd notice that it would happen more when no one was around or looking.

Now I thought love was unconditional so who cared if my "Grandpa Terry" hugged me and said he loved me. I'm just like his other grandkids I would say to myself. Well, this Sunday while hugging and doing a bit more rubbing than usual he asked me to come back over once everyone left for Church. Major red flag for me!

I knew it wasn't right. Why would he ask me to do that? I was a sheltered kid but not a dumb one. I knew I had to make noise so I got loud and kept asking, "Why do you want me to come back when they leave?" He was telling me to be quiet and I got louder. I remember abruptly leaving. Mama was at work so I was all alone on the couch crying. What would he have done to me had I went back?

This entire time was he being nice to take advantage

of a ten year old? I remember being balled up in the corner of the couch just crying and crying. I couldn't call Mama at work. She forbade me to so I had to sit in my own feelings for hours until she got home.

Dammit Dysfunction, just when I thought I found happiness and peace in my life after my best friend dies, here you come. It was at THAT MOMENT that my trust issues surfaced.

Mama gets home and I tell her. She is upset and asking questions. She says that she talked to him and explains to him that if anything ever happened to her child she'd kill whoever did it. I was not there. I don't know what happened or if it ever happened. I just know that after that, they remained friends and I distanced myself as much as I possibly could but I didn't want to hurt his wife so I kept it a secret.

After his wife died I never stepped foot in that house again. I had nothing to say to him and did not want to be around him in anyway. After his wife died my Mama started cooking for him since he didn't know how. Even prepared dinners upon his request. There went any trust I had for anybody. For the longest I couldn't even trust my own Mama!

Fast forward a few years into adulthood. I've gone through a crap load of bad relationships. I've been spat on, cheated on, lied to, lied about and everything in between. All I wanted to do was find the love that I thought was, "due me". The love that I lost when my Daddy left me.

One relationship after another is how I lived for a very long time and they were ALL spearheaded by none other than you, DYSFUNCTION. I just kept seeking "this thing" hoping it would fix me somehow. I have struggled to maintain positive relationships and friendships in my life. The death of every relationship and every friendship led me to question the love that I had for myself. At one point I didn't even love me anymore. I would ask myself, "Why should I when no one else does?"

At age 26, I was put on all kinds of medication to help me to cope. Heart meds, depression meds, anxiety meds, and something to help me sleep! Dysfunction you left me with nothing! Nothing but sleepless nights, horrible decisions, tears and questions. I was always taught that you go out and you treat people right. You treat them the way you'd like to be treated. I did that. I didn't do the bad things and the wrong things that many people I knew did. I tried to be the good little Catholic schoolgirl and it never stopped you. It never once stopped you from fucking with me!

The medication prescribed to me I just couldn't continue. The depression was too great. It made it worse. Now suicide had been added on my list of things to accomplish and by this time I have a daughter. I cannot let you win. I refuse to let you win! I cannot let anxiety rule my life. I had to fight tooth and nail to find me again. I changed my focus and began to learn about meditation. I found a therapist to talk to and I began to open up and I realized that those things that I thought were strengths were put in place as a defense mechanism against being hurt.

I did not want to be hurt again and before I experienced pain, I'd rather inflict it on you. There was no escaping it so then I figured a way to use it to my advantage. The only problem is I was continuing the hurt. I was inflicting pain on others just so I didn't have to feel it. I honestly even made a game out of it. Dysfunction, you are such a trickster.

You made me feel worthless but I know I'm not. You made me feel unlovable but I know I'm not. You made me feel like so many things were my fault but I know they weren't. It was you all along.

After so many years fighting with you Dysfunction I simply decided to walk away. I walked away from you and situations that no longer served me. Yeah, you try to rear your ugly head now but I'm stronger than you. You've put me through things I never thought I'd come out of and I did! Each time I did I was stronger and wiser and you became weaker and weaker!

Shortly after I began to REALLY work on me, my husband arrived. We had known each other since High School and he had been looking and asking around about little old me! I was shocked. Me?! Why me?! Let me be the first to say that he was and is a godsend. I'd like to think that my Daddy had a hand in this (thank you Daddy)!

My husband loves me unconditionally, he protects me, he nurtures me and most of all he listens to me and tries to understand. It hasn't been easy but I am learning how to communicate better. I'm learning how to turn off my defense mechanism and just be.

Emotionally, I've been a wreck most of my life. I've had trust issues most of my life and I dressed it up with fancy hairstyles, clothes, and cars and the only thing that matters and has ever mattered is the love that I reserve for myself.

Dysfunction, you may have won a few battles but trust me when I tell you that this war is mine....and I AM THE VICTOR! The control you had, you no longer have! The abuse you inflicted no longer works on me and I no longer work through you! You see Mama and I are getting along a lot better now don't you? That must upset you. Love found me too! Makes you mad doesn't it?

Oh, and remember when you had me thinking I was incapable of succeeding on my own terms? Well, I'm a business owner now and doing well so see, Dysfunction, no matter how long you stayed or how much work you did, when it was your time to go, it was time to go! You are not, nor will you ever be welcomed into my family home. My children will know nothing of you and I will teach them your signs and red flags so they too can avoid you at all costs.

You'll never win again and that's a promise,

Words of Wisdom and Love

Be confident about solving life's problems successfully through prayer, meditation and introspection. No longer look at those things that exist outside of yourself as a part of yourself. Understand that even though the world around you may be in chaos, you can still live in peace and that you deserve to do so.

AUTHOR'S BIO

Christina Jiles is a 36 year old Native of Houston, TX and is married to loving husband Quentin Jiles and proud Mother to both Ari (15) and Jae (14). She's the owner of small business **Nerdgirlchic Customized Pillows & More** and prides herself in family, entrepreneurship and overcoming life's obstacles in order to help others. Her motto is, "We're all in this together."

The Awakening

Teresa E. Mack

Dear Beloved,

I call you Beloved because now I realized that I have truly forgiven you. I no longer hold you totally responsible for the heartache and bondage that I experienced in our marriage. I now realize that if I had loved me enough I would not have allowed such behavior in my space. I can now pray that you find the same peace that I have found and that your life is full of joy and purpose. I can now say thank you without the jaded sarcasm and harsh feelings toward you. I appreciate you and all that I have learned from you. I have absolutely no regrets for marrying you.

Being married to you taught me to look deeper into self to see who I really was and who I could become. Although I didn't see it right away, over time, I realized that God kept me in the midst of all that I was experiencing for a reason and purpose. He gave me insight to who I could become if I focused on Him and not what I was experiencing. It wasn't an easy task. When I didn't feel loved by you, He was there showing me that I was worthy of His love. Being married to you also allowed me to see clearly the areas where I needed growth. There were some areas that I either refused to acknowledge or I just had no idea were problematic.

Let me explain:

I have realized that I had the fear of rejection. This fear, made me susceptible to accepting behavior that was beneath what God has for me. This fear made me believe that my happiness and peace were not important and that I had to focus on everyone else's happiness so that they would accept and not reject me. This fear put me in the company of needy and narcissistic people who used every opportunity to drain me of what little happiness that I had claimed. Leaving me depleted, drained and needing to be emotionally filled.

I had God and I knew that, but I felt so empty and felt myself emotionally vanishing from the life I claimed to be perfect. I felt that if I "faked" the good life long enough it would become my reality. I wanted it so desperately, and in my mind I was almost there.

That life, I now realize was just a shell of my delusions. Pseudo happiness is not happiness. I never expected to be 100% happy and have peace, because in my mind I never thought that it was possible for anyone to be that way, especially me. I had never seen anyone "that" happy or even at peace; so I thought I was fine.

Then I began to feel empty, and incidentally, I did what any carnal minded person would do; I looked for something or someone to fill that deep, dark void in my life. I was lonely, so lonely that I ached inside. The void that I initially thought was "normal" left me longing for peace. So I searched for the thing that I thought would complete me. I thought that I found that in you.

When I was younger I believed the fairy tales that a big strong knight in shining armor would come to rescue me and make my life perfect. Little did I know that that childhood image was the thing that directed my thoughts as an adult. When I met you, I saw you standing tall and erect like the knight I imagined, and I was a damsel in distress. I never saw you as someone broken who needed to be rescued too. I looked at your outer appearance and saw strength and pride. You looked so strong, as if nothing could defeat you.

Unfortunately, I never paid attention to the signs of brokenness and pain that became visible while we were dating. I never saw what was actually happening; I only saw what I wanted to see, because you were my knight.

When I began to acknowledge the inconsistencies in your words and your behavior, I realized that there was a problem: a serious problem. How did I get here? How did I allow you to inflict your pain and the burdens of your heart on me? My pain was a lot to bear, but then I accepted your pain as well. It was too much for one person to carry.

However, I didn't want to disappoint you so I elevated my wifely duties and did what I thought would make you happy, and that would make me happy, so I believed. I was a good woman and that's what you needed. Even though there were many times that I felt a need to get out of the marriage, I kept telling myself that I could make things better for you, for us.

Before we were married, I saw your anger and your aggression toward others, but I never saw it as a problem. I saw it as you feeling alone and needing to be loved and I knew that I could be who you needed me to be. Sure, you had your issues, but so did I, and no one's perfect. I didn't want to come off as a self righteous or judgmental person, so I allowed the behavior to continue feeling that things would get better as time went on. I believed in you, and based on the definition of love that I understood. I loved you and so I married you.

Needless to say; over time, as your anger escalated my need to make you happy increased as well. When your anger turned towards me, I began to cover up or mask my emotions and my pain hoping that the life that I imagined as my happily ever after would eventually get better. Now, I'm not insinuating that I was an innocent participant in this. As things began to unfold, and I saw that my marriage was not as I expected, I retaliated with anger and aggression as well.

All while trying to protect my beliefs that this marriage could work. I believed that two broken individuals could make a beautiful marriage, if they truly wanted it. It was my prayer that it would get better eventually, because God can fix anything. What I later realized was that the life I wanted was based on my childhood perception full of fantasy and illusion: it was "never" as I previously imagined.

It wasn't until you threw me on the bed, and put your hands around my neck and said, "I should kill you, right now", that I realized that I was an abused wife and you had been threatening to take my life on many occasions. I needed to escape before you decided to bring your thoughts to fruition; but my perception had me fooled and I felt trapped. I began to cry out to God and pray for a way out. I needed His help if I wanted to be made whole.

My focus shifted from trying to make you happy towards God. I began to concentrate on Him and what His purpose was for me. As my prayer life increased, I began to feel stronger spiritually and emotionally. I felt that there was hope. I truly felt His presence. Of course you did not approve of this new behavior in me; which made your threats become more frequent and more aggressive.

I prayed and asked God to either give me grace in this marriage or means of escape. Then I had a very graphic and detailed dream that let me know what I needed to do. I acted, believing that God would be my strength and my guide. I had this dream in 2004, shortly before I left the marriage. However, I penned this poem in 2014. I hadn't realized that for ten years I was still haunted by the memory of the past pain of my marriage to you.

After I wrote this poem, I literally felt a burden lift from my life. I now have the peace that I so desperately wanted and needed. As I share this poem with you, I can wholeheartedly say, I forgive you and pray that you are set free from your pain and burdens as well.

The Dream...

Awakened by the alarm of my heart,
I opened my eyes into the dark.

Random flashes in the night;
Emergency lights shining so bright.

I move forward to see what's at stake,
The closer I got I felt my heart break.

I saw him like an animal, cuffed and bound,
Bleeding, bruised and pinned to the ground.

He continued to fight with anger in his eyes,
Then he looked toward me with a look of despise.

He shouted to them, "You have the wrong man",
His "rights" were read as they helped him to stand.

He shouted aloud, "I'd never do her harm."
Then he said to the crowd, "Nothing to see here, it's a false
alarm."

41

Then he began to laugh as if a joke was told;
My heart broke as I watched this event unfold.

I tried to speak, but I was silent and still,
Because the next thing I saw gave a gut wrenching chill,

A black bag was carried out of my house,
"Who is that?"I said, in an excruciating shout.

My family stood with tears of disbelief,
I felt something strange as that black bag passed me.

As I continued to watch, I heard a Voice that said,
"Make haste NOW or your destiny will be dead."

My eyes tear-filled and my body felt weak,
As I listened to the Voice continue to speak.

"What you see before you is the enemy's plan,
It's meant to destroy you and you must take a stand.

This is your end, if you decide to stay,
But if you trust Me, I'll provide a way of escape.

Don't be afraid, I'm here, and here I'll always be,
Don't listen to doubt or fear; with Me you can be free.

Each day you'll grow stronger, and find it easier to stand,
Trust me now, Daughter, and take my hand.

I did not call you to this life of abuse,
But I can only restore you, if in Me you'd choose.

Choose life and love, and freedom from pain,
I'll be your Healer and Shelter from the rain.

In your dark moments, I'll be your Light and your Guide,
When you are lonely and afraid, in my Comfort you can hide.

In me, there's the Peace that you desire and seek,
I'll be your Strength in the moments that you feel weak.

When you lack, I will provide, no good thing I will withhold
For you, I have abundance and riches to behold.

Then I suddenly felt a violent shake,
"What is that?" I thought, "Is that an earthquake?"

It's over...

My eyes opened; yes, it was only a dream....
Then I see him staring and standing over me,

The look in his eyes, was anger and hate,
"He's angry already"...I sigh and think.

He began to complain that I kept him up all night,
He said that I tossed and turned like I was in a fight.

"I'm fine," I said. Though he didn't bother to ask,
He could care less about me or the dream I just had.

Then I stare at the wall as my eye released a tear,
No peace, no freedom, no refuge is found here.

A chance, a window, a way of escape,
Is all that I need God, before it's too late.

As he left for work, I heard the door slam,
"This life," I think, "cannot define who I am".

An abused wife is not in God's plan,
I cannot die at the hands of this man.

43

I want to be free from this heartache and pain,
This life, it's destroying me and I see no gain.

My God, please give me the strength that I need,
To walk away and not turn back, to live and be free.

This life and this experience is not a loss but a lesson,
I know my actions and strength will for someone be a blessing.

From the book, "This Life, He Speaks..."
(C) 2014 Teresa E. Mack

As a result of me finding this new sense of peace, I have identified with my gift and purpose. I have become someone who I never thought I could become. I am now a published author of two books of poetry. My first book, "The InHer Me" and my second book, "This Life, He Speaks..." has allowed me the freedom to also venture out and compose a dramatized spoken word CD sharing some of the poems in that book. I am blessed.

I am a believer that everything that we experience in life will help catapult us to another level in life. We just have to trust God to lead the way, and that is not easy, especially when you are used to doing your own thing. So I end this letter by saying, Thank you. If it were not for you, I don't think that I would have found out who I really was or who I could become.

Beloved, I truly pray that you have found peace in your life. This is an amazing journey that I am on. The love of God is so much more than my false perceptions; it really does give new life. Just trust Him.

A Greater You is Inside, 1 Corinthians 2:9

In peace and love,

Words of Wisdom of Love:

Life Experiences are never a loss;
but always a lesson.

AUTHOR'S BIO:

Teresa E. Mack is a Christian author from Baltimore, MD. She is a speaker, teacher and a poet. She enjoys sharing the Good News through her poetry and inspirational writings. She is a member of the Baltimore Chapter of The Maryland Writers Association, Christian Authors on Tour (CAOT) and the Johns Hopkins at Eastern Toastmasters Club.

Her first book, *The InHer Me, Thoughts and Poems from the Heart*, is a compilation of short stories, inspirational messages and poetry. Her second book of poetry, *This Life, He Speaks*, is a journey through her life experiences.

She is a devoted mother and a dedicated member of The New Psalmist Baptist Church in Baltimore, MD where she proudly serves on the New Member Ministry, the Discipleship Ministry and the Women's Ministry. She is also a contributing writer for Johns Hopkins University's Process Improvement Newsletter, the Harmony Hearsay.

She is a graduate of The University of Baltimore.

Her love for writing began at an early age and stems from her life experiences and intimate conversations with God.

Her poems have been featured in the nationwide Epitome Magazine, Maryland Writers Association Newsletter and the Johns Hopkins University's Harmony Hearsay Newsletter.

Connect with Teresa:

Facebook: Teresa E Mack – Author
Twitter: @TereMack
Instagram: teremack64
Email: freebeloveyou@gmail.com
www.amazon.com/author/teresamack

UnVolunteering My

Victimhood

✻

E. Chemeen Johnson

Dear Abusers,

I never saw myself as a killer; yep I fully and knowingly committed murder. I stabbed y'all with every ounce of my soul until you were dead. You bitches weren't easy to kill.

Y'all fought hard, like your life depended on it and it did but I fought harder. It wasn't a pretty battle either. It was bloody; I have scars to display proudly because it was a war worth fighting. To get to any of you, I had to take out your crew. One by one, kill by kill, stab by bloody stab. None of you were easy to take out either. Sometimes, I had to fight two or three of y'all together in different combinations. Some of you hoes I had to kill multiply times. It's like you were Jason from Friday the 13th or something. The dead became the undead, then they were alive again.

Shelba, you and your crew, Lolo, Ladajah, Procresha, Ditraya and Fressca are gone. I really had no other choice. To let any of you live would only cause me more pain. I killed not only for myself, but for the son that watches everything I do. See, once you had me you had him and that I couldn't stand for. Shelba, you and your gang were good but I was better. I couldn't do it alone though. I had help. My Daddy sent assistance. Anyway, today here I stand before you, victorious.

I just got tired of being tired of not living the full blessed life people always talk about. To have that life, I needed to change. I wanted, desired and prayed for change and nothing happened. I realized I needed to do more than just want.

The days, months and years passed me by wanting, and dreaming. I had read books, gone to seminars, gotten coaches and some progress was made. I was at a higher level of awareness. All this helped me come to the conclusion that I was my own abuser. No one could abuse me better than I could. I wouldn't allow another human to systematically do what I was doing to myself. I thought and talked more than I actually did. When I did do the work, things happened but something in me refused to do the work consistently.

Why couldn't I or wouldn't I do the work, I questioned?

There were biological reasons. I was diagnosed with hypothyroidism, which had me exhausted for years. After the diagnosis, I started taking my little white pill every day. This changed my life dramatically; I had the energy to live. I had energy to do more than work and sleep with a few events of living thrown in between. I literally had to retrain my body to stay awake after work.

I wasn't tired anymore but out of habit I felt the need to take a nap once I hit my home train station. I changed that behavior because it no longer suited the life I wanted to live. One would think after that nothing could stop me. Yet still no action was being taken. The beautiful thing about having a journal is being able to go back and read what was going on to help figure out what the real deal was.

I had no choice but to take drastic measures and so I did. If you haven't guessed, I killed what was in me, Self Sabotage aka Shelba. I gave all the behaviors within me that I had to kill names because I needed to personalize what I was dealing with. So allow me introduce you to the dead.

To Self-Sabotage aka Shelba,

You came to deliberately destroy, damage, and obstruct me from living my greatest and fullest life. You underhandedly interfered with the work I needed to do to succeed. Now you, bitch, are the leader of the bunch. Everything rolls up or down because of you but you never work alone. You just have your friends do the dirty work while you sit back and collect all the glory from their activities. Shelba, for so long, you have lived off of longings and unfulfilled desires. Such a master of disguise and deception. You're my last kill. My greatest kill. I cut your head off and danced on it in celebration.

On to your crew.

To Low Self-Esteem aka Lolo,

Lolo, you made me feel bad about being me I have felt unworthy, incapable, and incompetent. You had me so focused on what was wrong about me, I never saw any of the good in me.

To Laziness aka Ladajah,

You came in and got real comfortable. Slowly, little by little, stealing my energy and desire to do any work. Then you sucked all the life out and left me idle.

Procrastination aka Procresha,

You had me singing "Tomorrow, Tomorrow" until my relevancy was gone. You wanted me to just delay or postpone taking action. You made me lazy and took away my desire to do it now.

Distraction aka Ditraya,

You had me so wound up on the small insignificant stuff. I could never achieve those big goals or dreams because you had me going in twenty different directions. I never paid full attention to anything or anybody. You came in and eliminated my ability to concentrate. You are the one that blessed and cursed us all with social media.

Messing with you, Ditraya, is real tricky because you came in handy when the pressure was on and I needed a change to cope with a situation. Which isn't really an overall bad, bad thing? Sometimes I did need you to help me step back, breathe, do something else and come back to a situation. However, too much of you was my downfall.

To Fear of success aka Fressca,

Heifer, you here are a bittersweet weirdo because you're so appealing. Who doesn't want to be successful? A two-sided coin, with fear of failure being the other side. You did double duty giving and snatching dreams and goals in a heartbeat. Your requirement is that you change who you are and what you do, period. But I know change isn't change until it has changed. And you didn't want me to change.

What I know for sure is the time has come to tell the world what you have done to me. Today, I feel no shame, guilt or embarrassment because I am free. For me the price of freedom didn't come cheap. You know what the scariest part of the truth is: I wasn't your victim. I was a volunteer. No, I didn't raise my hand and choose what happened. I just merely went along with it and didn't resist at all. At this point being mad, hurt or angry is pointless. I only see the hero I am to have killed my own self sabotage.

Back to you, Shelba. One of your greatest assets is that I don't think I even know you. Yeah, we all have heard stories about what you did with so and so. But I never truly believed that you would do that to me. You are sneaky and deceptive. I didn't realize what you were doing until I got quiet, and went back to m saving grace of journaling.

Keeping track of my thoughts and inner craziness along with prayer started to reveal what was going on.

You showed up right after I submitted the documentation for my second co-author opportunity. I was nervous, but committed to see where this opportunity would take me. Yep, your girl E. Chemeen, is a number one bestselling author and budding speaker.

I did it!

I showed up and showed out. I basked in my own glory; I was living my childhood dream of having my name in a book. I was complete, or so I thought. This opportunity opened my mind to a new level of consciousness. I was exposed to a whole new level of being. I could not only be an author but have a profitable business writing. There was actually a process and system in place to make my dreams come true. It was all too much for my brain to process. As the days passed, and the seeds of possibilities started growing, so did your attacks of sabotage.

Journal Entry 5/21/15

Me – Did I seriously just rehash the "jump rope tragedy of third grade." (long story short, I was the new girl in a Black and Hispanic school. I had a jump rope nobody else did. My first contact was with the Latinas who claimed my recess jump rope privilege. My sistah girls weren't having it; I was Black and therefore belonged with that group. I was yelled at in Spanish then told I was ugly and they only wanted me for my rope. I sat alone at lunch for about two days. Then Kay, who was Black, came over and claimed my jump rope for her squad. She proceeded to enlighten me about my new neighborhood. I learned the housing project across from the school had SIDES. Literally who you hung out with depended on what side of the project street you lived on. Since I was new and lived in the private houses around the corner from the housing project, I was inducted by association.

Shelba – Yep, they never liked you, they only wanted to be your friend because you had a jump rope.

Me – Why am I thinking this, this is crazy. Where did that come from? I am done, good night!

The next morning, while praying, Self Sabotage was back with Low Self-Esteem.

Journal Entry 5/22/16

Me – Did I just interrupt my prayer to think about and rework the outcome of the "junior high, Ugliest to Prettiest List." (Short story: the guys in my school decided to rate the girls from ugliest to prettiest, I was number 22 on the list. I was crushed; out of 100 girls I should have at least ranged number 70-80's. I later found out I was cute but fat and that put me higher on the list.)

Lolo – You will never be good enough to be the prettiest on the list.

Me – What the What, I am praying. "Bless the pastors, their families and mine, Amen." I can't believe my prayer was interrupted for this craziness.

Shelba – You will never make it as a writer, who do you think you are?

Shelba & Lolo – You're really not that great of a writer. You will never master all of this technology. Why would anybody *pay you for the crap you write?*

Me – I am too damn grown for this. I am whole and healed. Lord please reveal what is going on with me.

Things got worse after that, I was bombarded with thought of the past along with all the new possibilities I saw for my life. My brain jumped from one extreme to the other. From I think I can, to it's totally impossible for me to do.

Journal Entry 5/24/15

Me – I am not sure what feels authentic enough to build my business platform on. Hmmm, what will I be known for??

Procresha & Ladajah (Procrastination and Laziness) – why you doing all this extra brain work? We will write down all these amazing ideas during the next commercial break. You just got home from working all day, you need a quick nap.

Me – No, not really, I am good. But I should relax a minute.

Ladajah – Ain't you just a little tired, ok don't take a nap. Just sit down and chill for a minute.

Procresha – You're a morning person, just get up at 4a.m. and take care of everything.

This head chatter was becoming an everyday thing.

Journal Entry 5/27/15

Ditraya (Distraction) – You can listen to your business coaching replays while watching TV. If anything important is said you will pick up on it.

Me – I really need to be serious about my health and

business aspirations. I don't think I am really showing up for my life the way I want to? I am not sure why?

Ditraya – Oh there is the periscope signal, let's see who is on now. You can always go back to the replays later. Before I do that, let me see what I am wearing to work tomorrow. You need to check your bank account to see if you have enough money to get your hair done.

Me – I feel like I am working in a circle. I start one thing, do half of it then move to another. I circle my kitchen table and one by one complete almost everything but never start and complete any one thing anymore? What is with that? Tomorrow I will consciously focus on one thing until it is complete.

What I realized the next day was I had to be present in my life, and conscious of my thoughts and actions. I had to diligently focus on what I wanted and what I was doing. In the beginning, it was difficult to do. I would start, do well for a few days and then fall off because I didn't stop any unproductive thoughts. That's when I realized the only way I could win was to be brutal. I needed to be brutally honest and disciplined with all aspects of my life that I wasn't happy with. This worked better than my other attempts, and lasted a few months, then as with most things in my life I began slacking. Shelba and her crew were at it again.

Journal Entry 9/2/15

Me – I see myself falling back into old patterns. I am not liking the direction I am going into at this time

Fressca (Fear of Success) – You are just doing too much. You will never be able to handle all the responsibility it takes to be a BUSINESSwoman. You have a pretty good life and doing more would require more than you can give.

Me – Huh if I am the owner I can create what I need to be, I can establish some type of balance.

Fressca – Now you know you can't maintain all that. You're not equipped for that level of life

Me – Hold up!! Wait! That is some real unloving shit, I am done!

Then I got really sick. I was in bed for four days. During this down time, I was able to get real clear on what I needed to do. I kept entertaining thoughts that needed to be cut off before they were able to take hold of my consciousness. So I went on a killing spree.

To kill both you, Lolo (Low Self-Esteem) and, Fressca (Fear of Success), this required a refusal to see myself as anything but great and amazing. I became so conceited with my love of self that no other thoughts could occupy space in my world. That's right, I suffocated you.

Lolo, I put my hand around your neck and squeezed until there was no life left. I gotta laugh because you revived yourself in several different disguises. You put in an assault on my body image. So I started exercising. Can't wish for a flat stomach and skinny thighs, you must work for them, so I did. No questions or discussion, just doing the work. Another attack came regarding my parenting skills. That was easy; just do my best every day. Bomb!! Don't entertain any negative crap.

Now Fressca, you were the fastest and easiest. I smothered you, with a pillow. Nothing beats a failure but a try. So I simply did it afraid. Step by step. I aligned myself with people who were doing what I want to do and did what felt right for me and my situation. No more mental chatter was acceptable. I had thought about things long enough.

Now my other kills were more intense because you all required both mental and physical work. To stop you, Procresha (Procrastination), I had to do whatever right in the moment or plan it along with the steps to get it done. No more putting anything off.

To kill you I had to chop you apart with an axe. Again, no words just work. When things seem too big, they just need to be broken down. In many cases I just needed to gather my tools, equipment and resources. That includes asking others for help, or accepting someone's generosity to do it for me. It may not be how I would have done it but it's done and off my list. I just say thank you and be happy.

Then Ladajah (Laziness), I killed parts of you when I killed Procresha (Procrastination) but I had to take things one step further. I took those parts and grinded them up with a wood chipper. This was more mental than physical. I learned I could build my energy with my thoughts. So my inner mantra is: I always have the energy for everything I desire to do, my joyfully and abundant life requires to fully live. I had lived the life of physical and mental exhaustion.

Every kill was a direct stab at you Shelba (Self-Sabotage) and you were bleeding and growing weaker. I knew it and so did you. I was able to prevent any other reincarnations or versions of you from entering into my life, by the faith in my Father's words.

Words like I came to give you truth and life; choose life. I am the head and not the tail. I am the lender not the borrower. I was tired of not believing my Father loved me unconditionally so I chose to completely believe He did. I no longer lived with doubt. I was determined to find out what would happen if I exercised true faith. I learned a long time ago that there was a level of protection in my Father's word. Like when He said "above all else guard your heart." It's so much easier to not allow things in my heart in the first place than to try and remove them You know I am talking about men right.

I knew that I had to kill you, Ditraya (Distraction) before I could take Shelba out because you, Shelba, were the umbrella that all these forces lived under. I was just so sick and tired of not shining as brightly as I felt inside. I was disgusted with not consistently doing the work necessary to achieve my the goals.

No amount of praying, wishing and hoping worked. I had to admit to myself I had a case of the NOTS, I did NOT because I did NOT. I was sick and tired. My process with myself couldn't be gentle because I don't operate like that with myself. Lord knows I wish I could but I can't. I can't allow any room for nonsense or renegotiation because I am just setting myself up for a slow decline, down to failure.

Now Ditraya, you were a slow kill, I actually had to ponder where I was sticking the knife in you. You probably died after the first 50 stabs but I needed about 2000 to really feel like the job was done. It took about 200 stabs to get over my Facebook habit, followed by 75 stabs for Periscope. Then there was television that took about 700 stabs, Ratchet TV by itself got about 250, followed closely by TMZ with 200, and home shows and Investigation TV got about 100 each. Y'all get the point. TV is a major distraction with me and robs me of my Author-preneurship and speaking business dreams.

Now that I had gotten rid of all my reasons, excuses and other Bull Crap, it was time to come back and address you, Shelba. This was not easy, because I had to look myself directly in the eyes.

Shelba – I was only trying to protect you from being crushed by judgmental people and their cruel comments. I know you say you don't care, but you do. I was protecting the little girl in you that can be hurt.

Me – I get that but I am grown, with moments of childish relapse. I know what to do to rescue me.

Shelba – You need me; I make sure you never go so far that you can't recover.

Me – I want to take the leap and fly. I can't do that with you weighing me down.

Shelba – What will you do without us?

Me – Go Big!! And with that I took out my Sword of Spirit and cut her head off. For this battle I put on The Full Armor of God. With my daddy all things are possible (Mark 10:27).

In conclusion, I had to kill all of you, all of the parts of me that were keeping me from living my purpose. I had to be prayed up and brutally honest with myself. I had to give up every bullshit excuse wrapped in good reasoning. I had to do the work!

A lot of this work had to do with me getting out of my own way. I had to forgive myself and others and not get caught up in my own feelings about the past. I had to stop dimming my own light because it made other people uncomfortable. I had to embrace compassion, kindness and not be so quick to get angry. I had to suspend my judgment of people and see them as works in progress that are as equally screwed up as I am. Above all that, I had to learn to love myself completely.

My life motto is "Forward is the motion, up is the direction."

I am my own beloved!,

E. Chemeen

Words of Wisdom and Love

"To Thy Own Self Be True."
Always be willing to tell yourself the total and complete truth
about the part you are playing in any given situation.
Then, if you don't like your answer, make a different choice.

AUTHOR'S BIO

Erica Che'meen Johnson is all about polishing the diamond that she is. E. Che'meen is an outspoken adventurous spirit with a flair for the dramatic. She is always open to the wondrous possibilities that life has to offer. Her fiery tenacity in approaching new experiences keeps her growing, developing and seeking her life's purpose. Her many outlets of expression are writing, reading, kickboxing, striptease classes and relaxing at the spa.

Fabulous New Life, vol. 1 is E. Che'meen's second co-author contribution, the first being Tavis Smiley's 2002 book *Keeping the Faith*. She will be making her third book contribution in 2016's *Women On A Mission, Sisterhood Stores* and fourth in 2017's *A Letter to My Abuser*. E. Che'meen is the proud mother of a fourteen year old son CJ and cat named Sandwich. Presently, E Che'meen has several fiction and nonfiction projects in the works and is building her public speaking resume.

E. Che'meen Johnson was born and raised in Brooklyn, New York. She is a third generation home grown property owner. For the past fifteen years, E. Che'meen has held both Residential and Commercial Property Management positions' throughout New York City's five boroughs. Real Estate allows E. Che'meen the opportunity to provide direct service to individuals, families and businesses by providing comfortable places for people to be, think and grow. Her first love has always been writing. Co-authoring four anthologies has allowed E. Che'meen to express her writing voice on a range of topics and hone her journalism skills. E. Che'meen graduated from Marymount College, Tarrytown with a Bachelor of Science in Business Administration.

My Misery is My Ministry

Lisa R. Lloyd

Dear Baby Daddy,

*W*hy did you stand before me and God and agree to Love Honor and Cherish me until death do us part? Why did you think I was going to submit solely to someone who wouldn't love me as Christ loves the church? Something was missing? Was it love or fascination or the fornication that drove us to try to make things right by getting married? Oh how can I forget: I was pregnant and you wanted to do the right thing as a man and a father. Sounds good but it wasn't good.

Why didn't you just walk away? You had the opportunity; everyone has choices. What drove you to make me your punching bag? The damage will never go away. You were desperate to leave home. Trapped, you desired freedom and took me along for the ride but you weren't ready to be a husband and father all in one breath. My three little boys trusted you and called you Daddy. They loved you but you didn't even know how to love yourself.

I desperately wanted to be accepted and loved by you and I wanted a strong man of God as the father of my boys. I wanted a perfect family, a perfect marriage, and love that was perfect. I wanted someone who would unconditionally love me with flaws and all but that was not my reality. You reminded me often that you did me a favor by marrying me, a damaged lady with one ex-husband and three little boys. You drilled in me that no one would accept me or ever love me because of my past that overshadowed me.

I trusted you. I had faith in you from day one. You talked to me about your dreams and visions and you seemed to be such a strong man, naturally and spiritually. As we settled in our first little apartment overseas with no friends and no family, the jealous rages and the constant complaints caused arguments every day. You always talked about committing suicide and taking us down with you. I didn't realize until now just how God covered us through the fears and all.

You continued to rip me apart through the years and somehow you always blamed me. It was always my fault that we lacked what we needed. It was my fault that you married a readymade family and couldn't explore the lust that lived in your heart. You were a broken little church boy who took on a rejected little church girl and we both were trapped in a world that we couldn't understand. Attempting to be parents when we really desperately needed the nurturing and guidance of our own parents. We lacked maturity and caused the children to grow up filled with fear, rejection and doubt.

To make yourself feel better, you denied me friends and you denied me the freedom of being my own individual. It was your way or no way at all. You kicked me across the floor. You demanded sex day and night, once with a knife at my throat and another time with a gun to my head. Was I scared or too ashamed to leave?

Do you remember, (you should because it is still very clear in my mind) the insecurities that you had when you forbade me to get the mail or open the curtains to our home and would leave me $5 on payday every week to stretch for myself and 5 little children? I wonder if it ever haunts you the nights your own son would cry and you forbade me to rock him and comfort him. Or what about the night you shoved me and losing my balance I fell down the flight of stairs that caused me to go in labor when I was pregnant with your daughter.

Do you remember when you uncontrollably whipped

the boys and I tried to stop you so you beat me with the belt instead? Of course you don't remember these things because you were perfect and everything you did had justification behind it resulting in it being my fault. Then you threatened to kill me if I tried to leave you. Honestly if it wasn't for my children, I felt that I would have been better off dead.

I dreamed of death, I hoped for death, I prayed for death and was very angry every morning I woke up and had to face reality all over again. I hated my life, I hated myself and I definitely hated you. Every touch and every sexual encounter made me sick. It definitely wasn't out of love but obligation and as you stated it was my duty. You watched porn and complained that I didn't fulfill your desires.

How could I?

After being belittled and criticized, pushed, punched, going to church with a black eye with lies that I fell, slapped and sometimes kicked, how could anyone lay in any position and give themselves to someone. Then you would bring flowers home and call all day saying you're sorry and then the cycle would repeat again. I was on the edge of a nervous breakdown trying to convince myself that suicide would be the answer but without forgiveness from God I was afraid to follow through.

Even now I am totally embarrassed and full of shame and guilt that I allowed myself and my children to sit in a world they call ABUSE. I was your little Black slave even though you called me your Brown Sugar. You controlled me as you stomped through the house screaming "I AM THE MAN, THIS IS MY HOUSE IT'S MY WAY OR NO WAY". Your prideful stern ways smelled in my nostrils like demons that crawled to torment a helpless soul.

I was totally faithful to you for many years regardless of the foolish allegations your mom always broadcasted. It is funny how miserable people try to make everyone miserable because they cannot face their own foolish past. Even your little secret affairs you thought I never knew about but I did.

Truth is, I didn't care. But in my lowliness when you stormed in the beauty shop screaming that it was taking too long, and that you didn't like my hair anyway, a gentleman overheard you. The shop was silent in disbelief of the verbal abuse you demonstrated. In the hour of my weakness, the gentleman who looked and heard the comments as he sat in front, came and wiped my tears and told me that I didn't deserve the dog treatment that you were giving. I fell into an affair with this man for over a year.

I was tired. I endured almost every kind of abuse. Emotional abuse, Mental abuse, Economic abuse, Sexual abuse and Physical abuse for over 13 years in a dead end cycle. It is funny how you ran from person to person and church to church discussing the affair without mentioning your own multiple affairs and the abuse I suffered for years.

It's ok. I turned my misery into ministry informing the world that we as women matter and abuse of any kind is wrong and not tolerated by law. I urged many women with children to put themselves and their children first and that two wrongs never make a right. I stepped outside my marriage initially and I was totally wrong. I sinned before God and disrespected you as my husband and children. So you did not destroy me. I am very strong and I now have the testimony of an overcomer, a survivor and a minister of my Misery.

For years, I hated you praying that you would die. For years, I had regret. For years, forgiveness was not an option, but I thanked you for your apology.

However, I cannot understand why you continue to embrace every opportunity you have to put me down and taint my character. Please live your life. You had a girlfriend before we separated, you lived with her and her mom before the divorce, you married her right after the final decree so enjoy your life. Please embrace what you have and be happy. STOP using your regrets to reprove me. I am happy and doing well and help many women who have fallen in the stink I once was in. I am ministering to the miserable using my own testimony as my guide.

A Baby Daddy, a man that placed a seed and never embraced the seed or the seed carrier.

But, I survived.

Your Baby Mama,

Lisa R. Lloyd

Words of Wisdom and Love

In pondering for words of wisdom and love to give, I thought about the master and His Master plan and the many words of wisdom that he has provided in the word of God knowing that God is Love, and Love is GOD. It is impossible to have God and not have Love.

For God so loved the world that He gave His only begotten son that whosoever believe in Him shall not perish but have everlasting LIFE. So I introduce to some and present to others the Man of Wisdom and Love my Savior Jesus Christ. In Him I have developed into a Kingdom Ambassador in all my ways I acknowledge Him and He directs my path.

In a life as a caterpillar for many years, feeling ugly and worthless with no desire to live, I embraced my Abba Father as I accepted the embrace that He offered me for many years. I casted all my cares on Him and He wiped every tear from my eyes. In Him I live and breathe He is the source that I abide day after day. The process was not easy.

There were many stages and many falls but I broke free from the cocoon I lived in and developed into a butterfly. No longer am I living by the thoughts of others, but the thoughts He has towards me. I had to learn to love God totally, then love myself, which allowed me to love others not only as a healed individual but a whole woman strong and victorious in Him. Words of Wisdom and Love I give is to Confess with your mouth and believe in your heart.

AUTHOR'S BIO

Lisa R. Lloyd a wife, mother, grandmother, pastor, author, mentor, speaker, entrepreneur and domestic violence advocate was born in Maywood, Illinois. She launched her first book *Rejected by my Daddy and Embraced by my Father* in September 5, 2013. A year later, Lisa created a play by the same name that hit the stage to a sold out audience. Her book, *Caterpillar to the Butterfly* was published April 1, 2015 and her third book *Contaminated Fruit* is due to come out December of 2016. Lisa has also contributed a chapter in an upcoming book entitled *A Letter to My Abuser Once a Victim Forever Victorious* by author Sharisa Robertson.

Lisa and her husband Kevin Lloyd were ordained as Pastors June 1, 2014 and founded Anointed with Purpose and Destiny Worship Center. Pastor Lisa and Pastor Kevin are now active members of Christ Family Worship Center under the leadership of Apostle Royal and Apostle Kimberly McClinton where they are both in ministerial training. Lisa received her Associate Degree in Bible Studies and Pastoral Ministries in 2016 from Ohio Christian University in Circleville, Ohio. Fashioned with Favor, her hobby turned business, further showcases Lisa's creative side.

Lisa has endured abuse on many levels and is an overcomer. This is what makes her passionate about helping women learn to love themselves while uplifting and encouraging them to know that the cycle of abuse can be broken. Lisa plans to relaunch, *Rejected by my Daddy and Embraced by my Father* along with a 30 Day Journal June 2017.

Lisa's mantra is "I am a citizen of the Kingdom of God and He alone do I serve."

Abuse is Abuse is Abuse

✖

Sharisa T. Robertson

Dear Familial Abuse,

*T*his is going to be not so sweet and straight to the point. I don't know when you penetrated yourself into my family, but you have become such a regular, normal way of living. You take no prisoners and anybody under your influence can be used to hurt others or be hurt by you; mothers, fathers, cousins, siblings, aunties, uncles, grandparents.

I grew up around you. I have experienced you, felt you, feared you, been bound by you. You are so familiar that you've been ingrained into families, becoming a part of them, who they are, what they do, and how they act. Expected even. I despise how families are built around you without question. I despise your disregard for families causing family members to disregard each other.

From your perspective, you are actually smart. Family, is hard to break free from because family is all you got, right? Familial abuse is so hard to point out, let alone speak out against, especially when dealing with certain relationships. And for some reason, the person who speaks out, is usually the person who is outcast, talked about, forced to forgive, and frowned upon, not the abuse or abuser.

You've distorted the meaning of blood being thicker than water. So clever. Many families are used to the abuse, they want to forget it, they don't want to talk about it. Then, the one doing the abuse, acts like the one they abused is supposed to take them for who they are, walk on eggshells, develop tough skin and again get over it, no matter how painful the "it" is and how many times and ways they hurt us.

You bring in yo' "peoples" (verbal, mental, emotional, psychological, sexual, financial, and spiritual, abuse) and destroy bonds, memories, relationships, gatherings, people, communities, mindsets, generations, even talents. Because, to destroy a family, you have to break down the people in it, one at a time. Robbing them of each other and of themselves. Consume them and give them no hope or healing, that they become so overwhelmed they spill it out unto others and the others, take it, as if, you are their birthright.

I have been abused and have abused. I have gossiped, argued, fought, tried to fight, sat silently watching abuse of some sort, not speak up for myself when I should. I have mistreated my children and loved ones with my words and actions, knowing I was hurting them to their core because I was so overwhelmed and emotionally disconnected, I became cold to those who only tried to love me. And on the flip side, trying to show my love by allowing others to dump on me, thinking I was strong enough to handle the pain that they couldn't handle.

But, isn't that how you work?

You prey on the broken hearted, the overwhelmed, the stressed, the wounded, the ones that can't face their pain, their feelings, that try to jump straight to being strong that they neglect to care for themselves. Those that have been hurt many times, they become so bitter, so resentful that they hurt others so no one can hurt them or see their hurt.

But I see the pain. I understand why we all do what we do. Although it doesn't make it right, to understand is a start. I know you've definitely broke me down but what you didn't realize that while I was down, I was able to gain my composure and break free. Free from you, free from the dysfunction, free from distorted views of normalcy. The more you have a hold on some, the more I have to back away. I know now that it is not ok, it is not healthy, it doesn't hurt less because it is family, it hurts even more.

It is just as abusive to witness someone being subjected to abuse but not say anything because you don't want to start something or you are scared to speak out. It is abusive (although many don't even realize it) to ask someone to tolerate the mess for whatever reason. It is abusive to apologize and then do it again. It is abusive to ostracize someone for not wanting to take part of any of it anymore. It is abusive to ask someone to be around their abuser, in spite their discomfort and in spite of the abuser's wrong doings and lack of accountability. It is abusive to coerce people to stay in an abusive familial relationship and throw all the weight on them, yet if it were an outsider you would encourage them to not accept that mess. It is abusive to teach this directly and indirectly to generation after generation, perpetuating the abuse.

I have always let you win for the sake of family, for the sake of the holidays, for the sake of letting them be and just ignore them because you know how they are, for the sake of what they may be going through, for the sake of who they were to me, for the sake of what they may have done for me, for the sake of what if somebody was to die, all while I was dying inside. I took all of that into consideration but when the "ish" hit the fan, for whatever reason, no one has the same consideration for me.

So I know the saying is, what happens in this family, stays in this family but when it comes to you, I no longer adhere to that. I will no longer hide or share you. I can't choose family and I can't choose what they do, but I choose what I tolerate, sugarcoat, battle with. I accept you. I accept them. But I will not force myself to accept any mistreatment.

I will heal and help others heal. I will feel the pain you've caused and turn it into my purpose. I will trust myself, forgive myself, decide if and when I will forgive others and move on with life.

I will write, speak out about you, even if it means making things even more strained in my own family. I will confront you, scared and all. Whether it is you coming against me or I witness someone being subjected to you through another family member. The truth will set us all free, if we let it.

I will destroy all generational curses and dysfunctions you appear as by understanding you and use what I have learned about you to dismantle your structures and systems. I will find the function in your dysfunction.

I will not hold anyone, in relation to me, in a higher regard than who I am to myself and my well-being. I won't listen to others say "I went through the same thing" or "it happened to me" or "it isn't that bad", as if I am wrong for having my own standard and enforcing it.

I will do more feeling and communicating and I will teach my children to do the same. I notice that you are able to thrive in families that don't talk and hide their feelings. I will advocate for my children and not abuse them in any way or let other family members abuse them. They will know abuse is unacceptable even when done by a family member. I will not subject my children to you anymore. I will teach them how you work through loved ones with no regard.

I will always, even from afar, love my family and hold on to the good memories and learn from the bad. I decide what defines family and will create a new family paradigm that aligns with my beliefs, values, feelings, desires, and purpose. It will not fit the world's view nor your view.

I am too good for you and I hope my family and other families begin to know that too. I pray for all families to be free of the abuse they bring to each other, especially my own. But I reject you and leave you where you're at and create a family of my own that don't play that shit you bring. I speak a divine healing so transformational, so generation changing, so great, so purifying, to my family and to all families. And maybe one day, we will all love ourselves so much that we can love each other to your oblivion that families go beyond the appearance of everything being ok to being ok.

This battle you may have won, because some relationships have been severed but you have not won the war.

Giving you both middle fingers,

Words of Wisdom and Love

Abuse and violence in family does exist. If you're being abused in any way by anyone in your family, know you are not obligated to put up with it for the sake of family.
Know for your family to hurt you, they had to have been hurt themselves first, and that hurt has never been dealt with.
With that said, understand it but don't excuse it.
You are not a doormat, punching bag, or a trash can.
Break all brooms and lift up all rugs and no longer participate in family secrets, dysfunctions and abuse by sweeping shit under the rug.
You were not created to abuse or be abused.
Love whomever from afar.
Set clear boundaries.
Enforce them.
Depart from whoever if you have to.
Put you first.
And heal to make space for whatever is next.

Author's Bio

Sharisa T. Robertson is the founder of **Emotional Activism Worldwide, LLC** and **Lilies of the Field Media, LLC**. Sharisa debut as an co-author in *Cheers of Your Success: Women on the Rise and Owning their Destiny* (by Carol Sankar). Since then, she was inspired by the healing artistry of sharing your story and turning your pain into purpose.

She is the author of *A Daughter's Struggle, A Daughter's Success: How to Honor Yourself while in a Strained Relationship with Your Mother, Hard Truth, Healing Truths: 120 Perspectives to Make Shift Happen in Your Life*, and *The Realest Shift Ever Felt: Changing the Way You Feel about Your Feelings*. She is also the visionary of book collaborations, *A Letter To My Mother: A Daughter's Perspective, A Letter To My Bully: Sticks, Stones, and Words Do Hurt*, and *A Letter To My Abuser: Once a Victim, Forever Victorious*.

Writing since she was 10, Sharisa had over 100 episodes of her own TV show written and all on her paper, making her room a fire hazard. After constantly hearing about the starving artist, she made up her mind that it would be impossible to try and actually pursue a career in writing. Although she still wrote in her journal, loved to take notes, and wrote in her calendar, her passion for writing was pushed aside and she gave it up, only writing on occasion. So, to be an author and a businesswoman over 20 years later, is a dream come true.

Sticks and Stones

Miss Buttafly

To All The Men I've Allowed To Speak Over Me,

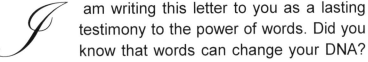 am writing this letter to you as a lasting testimony to the power of words. Did you know that words can change your DNA? That means that we can upgrade or downgrade ourselves physically, emotionally, and spiritually by the words we speak. Even the Bible says that "death and life are in the power of the tongue." So, I am overwriting all of the negative programming created by your words borne from pain.

Because I loved, respected, and valued you as father, brother, friend, and lover, I allowed you to speak terrible words filled with guile over my life and into my spirit. I trusted you to endue me with powerful masculine magic, but instead all you did was vomit your pain all over my soul with words that should've been sweeter.

This letter will be the last time I recall these words. It will be the last time I give any of my energy over to your poison. With this letter, I return all of your shame, guilt, angst, and low self-esteem to their rightful owners.

And please, don't get it twisted. This is not about blame. I love myself too much to place blame on anyone. No, this is about freedom, MY freedom. What you will read here is a reflection of how YOU felt and may even still feel about YOU. I've carried your words inside my head for too long. That ends now.

So, now that we're clear Let us begin.

"You out here whoring around with these strange boys doing God knows what!"

I was 14. Fourteen years old and had never been touched. And you called me a whore. For getting a ride home. What made me a whore, Dad? Was it because the young man who gave me the ride was 18? Or was it because he gave me a ride home in a van? Can you imagine what it felt like to be called a whore by your father? Have you ever been exposed to the vitriol that can come from your own mouth? The only thing that hurt worse than you calling me a whore was the slap to the face that came after... Damn, Daddy.

You were supposed to protect me, to shield me from all hurt, harm, and danger. But you didn't. How could you when the danger was you? Dad, the way you spoke to me convinced me at one point that you hated me. I mean, I legitimately thought you despised my existence. Of course, I know better now because we have healed to some degree. However, the deeper I heal, the more I realize that much of what I called low self-esteem was really just the program you installed with your often cruel words. It wasn't me that you hated, it was you.

Dad, I love you, but those words do not belong to me anymore. You can have them back.

"No man wants a girl who's smarter than them. You'll have to dumb down and take one for the team because you intimidate men."

Your words were supposed to sow seeds of power and grace and confidence into the lush, fertile soil of my soul. Instead, you used your words to plant stinkweed. The weight of your words was heavy like a bag of rocks. They sank into me and left holes where flowers once grew.

You made me feel as if I was undeserving of a love, of a life, that was free and beautiful. You made me feel like free and beautiful was something that could never be mine, like I would always be a prisoner to mediocrity. Your words made feel like being intelligent was a curse that made me an undesirable mate. You spoke to me as if you hated me, and I often think you did.

You knew what dating was like for me and how important it was at the time for me to be in a healthy relationship. You even shared some of the same woes. Yet, you chose to use your words to fondle my pain. Telling me, an intelligent Black woman, to lower the demonstration of her intellectual capacity is not love. It is not friendship. It is an act of warfare against Black womanhood.

So, where I once saw you as a brother, I now know you to be a traitor. You cannot be trusted. Take your words back.

"You might as well marry him because you already have two children by two different men, and who gon' want you."

I did marry him, Dad. He divorced me 18 months later and another baby later. He told me that he regretted marrying me and that it was the worse decision of his life. See what your words co-created? I took your fatherly advice and married a man who I knew didn't really love me. And it failed, miserably. You knew that his intentions weren't pure. Yet, you encouraged me to marry him because being a mother of 2 children who have different fathers somehow made me... what? Used up? Invaluable? A waste? Unworthy to choose or to be chosen?

Man, I know I've said it before, but I think you hated me because I reminded you of you, so you tried to turn me against my own soul with your words. And it almost worked... Almost. How painful it must have been for you to see the light that illuminated your darkness! To see those things within yourself that you wanted to hide being brought into the light must have been torturous for you. So, you spoke what you felt, projecting it into me, hoping that that would somehow ease the pain of your own conscience. You tried it. You really did.

The good news is that I don't hate you, at all. I still love you very much. I mean, you're my Daddy. But... you can have these words back.

"If we break up and I find out you're talking to one of my friends, I'll kill you."

You threatened to kill me. Oh, I know that you'll say that you didn't, but you did. The funny thing is that it isn't surprising that you would resort to violent language to prove your point. That's how it went, right? We would fight, and you would begin hurling out slurs and cruelties. It was the way you were taught to miscommunicate.

I don't blame you. I know your people. I have experienced the cacophony of violent words that is your family. I don't blame you, but I don't excuse your participating in such savage behavior either. You used your words against me in anger as weapons of mass destruction. You bombarded my soul and my body with verbal missile strikes and raided my emotional coffers with threats of violence and words like "bitch" and "hoe." You attacked me the way a frightened, starving, wounded animal attacks anyone who tries to offer it food, wildly and without care.

"I should've never tried to turn a hoe into a housewife."

You said this to me after I broke up with you and rejected your advances to continue having sex. You said you didn't care, that it was just sex. But it was clear that you cared, even if it wasn't for me. You cared about your woundedness. You cared about your ego. You cared about the perceived slights against you. You cared about the heaven between my thighs that you felt entitled to. It didn't matter to you that you had wounded me. It was all about you, and that's all that mattered.

Well, since your pain matters so much to you, sir. Here are your words back.

"You look like you can suck a mean dick."

I asked you how. You said because the corners of my mouth curl when I smile. I thought we were close like brother and sister. I thought you actually respected me as a friend and colleague. It was clear to me what you saw when you looked at me. To you, brother, I was a thing, an object to be consumed. Instead of telling me how powerfully I speak or complimenting me on my command of the English language, you told me my mouth was meant for one thing. You tried to lessen me, brother. You were completely out of pocket to even fix your lips to say that to someone you once called sister. I thought we were family.

Your words picked at old scars that hadn't quite healed yet. I shared my story in confidence and exposed my vulnerability to you as a sister would to a brother. And all you could think about was how my lips would look wrapped around your penis. It hurt... at first. Then, I realized something.. You weren't my brother at all.

You can have your words back.

"Shhhh... Don't tell anybody. They won't believe you anyway."

85

Famous last words... Whispered after calloused hands had left their ashy marks on pristine flesh. I was a child, a girl, and innocent. And these words, these cold, few words silenced me for many years. I know why you said them, because no one believed you. No one heard you when you were screaming for your abuser to stop, so you told me the same thing when you became my abuser. But, it was a lie. It was a lie.

Someone did hear me and believe me and fight for me. Me. I heard my cries. I believed my experiences. I honored my truth. I healed. From every word that you spoke, and every piece of my soul that you tried to snatch away, I healed and am still healing. I will always heal from these ugly spells cast by forked tongues. Healing is the final word over my life.

Your words have forced me to a place of brokenness and deep introspection. I have come to learn that I AM whatever I say I AM. I have come to accept the truth that no matter what you or any other person on this planet says about me or to me, that it is NOT a reflection of me, but rather a reflection of them. I am on my journey to inner peace. That's why it was so important for me to give you these words back. Words are magic; that's why it's called spelling. And these spells are broken.

I choose to vibrate at the highest frequency possible. I choose forgiveness and freedom. I choose me.

I Speak Life!,

Words of Wisdom and Love

How to heal from verbal abuse:

The primary piece of advice I would give to any person who is dealing with a verbally abusive relationship is to trust your intuition. Intuition is the gift that is common to all people. Many of us, especially women, are taught to ignore our intuitive cues in relationships. We are taught to keep quiet and to go with the flow. We are taught that we cannot be trusted with our own agency and that our voice does not matter. Therefore, it becomes easy to ingest the toxic sludge that comes from a verbally abusive loved one.
Your intuition is your God-given gift. It is that "something" that always knows what is true and what isn't. When you strengthen your relationship with your intuitive voice, you will become less attractive to verbally abusive people. Villains need victims, and victims are superheroes who have forgotten their power.
Sit with yourself and listen. Learn to discern between voices that are not yours and that which is the true voice of your soul. Develop a practice of listening to yourself. Trust your gift. And do not allow anyone in your space who violates your soul.

"No one can make you feel inferior without your consent."
– Eleanor Roosevelt

"Death and life are in the power of the tongue."
- Proverbs 18:21 KJV

"When people show you who they are, believe them."
– Maya Angelou

"You are powerful beyond measure."
– Miss Buttafly

AUTHOR'S BIO

Dr. Dionne S. Wood is the founder of the **Temple of the Sacred Spring** and iWorshipHer.com, an online community and lifestyle blog for WOC focusing on body, soul/spirit, and mind. As an empath, a clairvoyant, and a minister, Dionne, better known to the online community as Miss Buttafly, is here to inspire women to take their gifts off the shelf, unwrap them, and put them on. Dionne seeks to empower women to embody their S.I.N.F.U.L. (Sensual. Intuitive. Natural. Free. Unashamed. Loving) nature. Dionne has been called a prolific orator, speaking truth to power. This multi-faceted woman has traveled across the United States, bringing her unique and relatable style of storytelling to a variety of audiences. Her energetic and humorous delivery will both captivate the imagination and challenge the mind to expand.

- Bowie State University, Psychology – 1993
- Trinity University, Human Relations – 2003
- Licensed as an evangelist in 2002
- Created LadyMinista Enterprises in 2005
- Author of Behold, The Dreamer Cometh published in 2005
- Founder/Instructor of Daughters of Destiny Leadership Institute in 2006
- Owner, Simply Elegant Affairs – 2006
- Ordained as a pastor in 2007 • {Honorary} Doctorate of Divinity in Biblical Studies conferred in 2008
- Strayer University, Business Administration – 2011

Afterword

You have heard the story of pain. Some of you have even had to tell it. In each of these letters you heard, felt, and may have even related to the depth of trauma experienced, but you also heard the triumph. These letters teach us all how to access words of wisdom that will help us reclaim our victory. These letters teach us how to change our stories and therefore change our lives. What every woman shared with you in this book is a blueprint on how to take some of the darkest moments in your life and shine the light of hope.

You, too, get to decide the impact of your experience. You cannot control everything that knocks on the door of your life, but you absolutely get to choose how it will impact you. Turn your pain into peace. Know that no matter what it is that you have been through, you are forever victorious and you are no longer a victim. What may have been taken from you, was never really stolen. You are not what happened to you. Within you is a power so great, that not even your abuser could not access it. May you conclude this book with a new perspective of who you are; you, my love, are victorious!

Thema Azize Serwa

The Womb Sauna
www.thewombsauna.com

90

Resource Section

Statistics

- Up to 70 percent of women experience physical or sexual violence from men in their lifetime — the majority by husbands, intimate partners or someone they know
- Worldwide, up to 50 percent of sexual assaults are committed against girls under 16.
- As many as 1 in 4 women experience physical and/or sexual violence during pregnancy which increases the likelihood of having a miscarriage, stillbirth and abortion.
- Every year 5,000 women are murdered by their relatives to protect the "honor" of the family
- Women who are beaten by their partners are 48 per cent more likely to be infected with HIV/AIDS because violence can negatively affect women's physical, mental, sexual and reproductive health, and may increase vulnerability to HIV
- Physical, mental, and sexual and reproductive health effects have been linked with intimate partner violence including adolescent pregnancy, unintended pregnancy in general, miscarriage, stillbirth, intrauterine hemorrhage, nutritional deficiency, abdominal pain and other gastrointestinal problems, neurological disorders, chronic pain, disability, anxiety and post-traumatic stress disorder (PTSD), as well as non communicable diseases such as hypertension, cancer and cardiovascular diseases. Victims of domestic violence are also at higher risk for developing addictions to alcohol, tobacco, or drugs

- 2.5 million people are trafficked annually into situations including prostitution, forced labor, slavery or servitude. Women and girls account for about 80 per cent of the detected victims.
- Worldwide, almost one third (30%) of women who have been in a relationship report that they have experienced some form of physical and/or sexual violence by their intimate partner in their lifetime.
- Globally, as many as 38% of murders of women are committed by a male intimate partner.
- On a typical day, there are more than 20,000 phone calls placed to domestic violence hotlines nationwide.
- The presence of a gun in a domestic violence situation increases the risk of homicide by 500%
- Studies suggest that there is a relationship between intimate partner violence and depression and suicidal behavior
- Between 21-60% of victims of intimate partner violence lose their jobs due to reasons stemming from the abuse.[6]
- Between 2003 and 2008, 142 women were murdered in their workplace by their abuser, 78% of women killed in the workplace during this time frame
- Between 21-60% of victims of intimate partner violence lose their jobs due to reasons stemming from the abuse.
- Between 2003 and 2008, 142 women were murdered in their workplace by their abuser, 78% of women killed in the workplace during this time frame.
- 19.3 million women and 5.1 million men in the United States have been stalked in their lifetime.[1] 60.8% of female stalking victims

- 1 in 5 women in the United States has been raped in their lifetime.
- Almost half of female (46.7%) victims of rape in the United States were raped by an acquaintance
- 45.4% of female rape victims were raped by an intimate partner.
- 8,000,000 is the number of days of paid work women lose every year because of the abuse perpetrated against them by current or former male partners. This loss is equivalent to over 32,000 full-time jobs
- Women who earn 65% or more of their households' income are more likely to be psychologically abused than women who learn less than 65% of their households' income.
- 98% of financial abuse that occurs in all domestic violence cases.
- Approximately 6 out of 10 Americans strongly agree that the lack of money and a steady income is often a challenge faced by a survivor of domestic violence when leaving her/his abuser.
- $948 is the average cost of emergency care for intimate partner violence related incidents for women. The average cost for men is $387.
- 79% of women experience workplace sexual harassment
- 48.4% of women have experienced at least one psychologically aggressive behavior by an intimate partner.
- 4 in 10 women have experienced at least one form of coercive control by an intimate partner in their lifetime.
- 17.9% of women have experienced a situation where an intimate partner tried to keep them from seeing family and friends.
- 18.7% of women have experienced threats of physical

harm by an intimate partner.

- 3/4 of the victims of family violence were female, about 3/4 of the persons who committed family violence were male.
- Family members were responsible for 43% of female murders
- Nearly half of all the family violence offenders in State prisons were serving a sentence for a sex offense against a family member

Types of Abuse

Abuse does not look, sound, feel, or is demonstrated as one way. It can be parental, relational, from a stranger, take place in the workplace, church, from a friend or associate, at school, at the doctor's office, at a neighbor's house, etc. It can take place from a man or woman, even in youth. Men, women, and children can be victims of abuse.

Abuse can also be done under the guise of sexism, racism, classism, colorism, and be systematic. It can also be self-inflicted or dysfunctional. It can also takes place online or using technology as well. Abuse is not limited to what is on this list. It is inappropriate and a violation and mistreatment of your rights, respectability, safety, values, spirit, soul, body and well-being. If it don't feel right (in any aspect), then it isn't right.

Emotional/Verbal/Mental/Psychological Abuse is:
- Name calling
- Put downs
- Threats of suicide
- Ignoring
- Intimidation
- Erratic and unpredictable behavior/responses
- Manipulation, corrosion
- Lack of emotional warmth/being emotional unavailability
- Attacks on character
- No regard for feelings/harsh judgment on other's feelings

- Overly dependent
- Playing the victim
- Yelled at
- Insulted
- Taunted/teased
- Slander
- Withholding responses, words, information
- Accusing/blaming
- Undermining comments that can be loud and obvious or quiet and not so obvious
- Countering (very argumentative)
- Discounting (denying the right to thoughts and feelings as true)
- Lied to or lied on
- Mocking
- Belittlement
- Forcing you to do degrading things
- Breaking promises, lack of responsibility

Social Abuse is:

- using the power of the group to intentionally embarrass and intimidate in front of others
- isolation from friends and family
- pushing groupthink
- bullying
- confining person to a room or place
- preventing participation in activities in and out of home
- stalking
- taking possessions or preventing to access to phone, internet, transportation, etc
- monitoring and controlling use of transportation, phone, internet, etc

- spreading rumors/lies
- telling personal business as a means to shame someone

Physical Abuse:

- Choking
- Hitting/punching/slapping
- Pushing
- Throw around
- Beaten/hit with objects
- Biting
- Pinching
- Hitting walls
- Spitting
- Shaking
- Touching inappropriately
- Pulling hair, body, clothes
- Restraining
- Burning, poking, twisting body parts
- Chasing
- Tackling

Spiritual Abuse:

- Create a dependence to one person for spiritual knowledge
- Demand blind servitude and loyalty from followers
- Uses authority, gifts, and title to control
- Uses position of trust for sex, sexual favors, or even to sexually harass
- Dominate and mind control others under the name of God or a Higher Power
- Outcast/bad mouth/blackball someone from church

- Constant demand of excessive and unreasonable time, money from followers
- Wanting to be first over followers family, job, responsibilities, etc
- Using the faith of another to wrongly persuade or manipulate
- Leadership that only have people who are allegiance with them, doesn't want or allow other ways of thinking that differs, challenges, questions them
- Uses cliques as a way to create a sense of prestige and important while looking down at those outside of the clique
- Creates an environment of fear and shame
- Use, treat as a slave or servant, mistreat, those that under leadership
- Leaders wanting to be consulted over every major decision of another's personal life
- Being told or asked to do things that doesn't aligns with beliefs, values, faith
- Demean someone instead of effectively correcting
- Feeling beat down, drained, after service
- Speaking own thoughts and words that are not of God but saying they are

Financial/Economical Abuse:

- Preventing you from having or keeping a job
- Interfering with your efforts to maintain a job by sabotaging childcare, transportation, or other arrangements
- Harassing you at work
- Controlling money and possession
- Using gifts to make up for abuse
- Taking your money

- Forcing you to ask others for money
- Excluding from financial decisions
- Refusing to work or withholding money,
- Not contribute you to financial responsibilities
- Is systematic abuse
- Forcing you to open accounts
- Not allowing name on accounts or access to money
- Demanding an account of purchases/account
- Boasting of being the breadwinner constantly and putting down your financial contribution as if it is nothing

Sexual Abuse:

- Inappropriate touching, contact (groping, fondling, kissing, rubbing, penetration, etc) of any body part (molestation)
- Demanding sex in exchange for favors
- Forced sex, sexual acts, sexual contact (rape, includes marital rape, incest as well)
- Human trafficking/pimping/forcing to have sex with another/solicitation of minors via internet
- Using sex as manipulation
- Indecent exposure of body parts
- Using position of trust to coercive, persuade, manipulate into having sex, forced sex or sexual acts, molestation
- Consensual sex that turned violent or brings harm, duress without the other's consent
- Possession of child pornography
- Peeping at someone
- Recording sexual acts, someone dressing/undressing, etc without consent for personal

use and/or the internet
- Solicitation
- Sexual harassment
- Consensual sex that turns non consensual and forced
- Uses drugs or alcohol to facilitate into sex
- Forcible object penetration
- Forcing someone to sexually touch, have sex, or perform sexual acts on another person without consent
- Kiss without consent

Living After Abuse

These are thoughts, feelings, and actions to do after abuse. The after can be just as hard as the during as you are coming into and back to yourself and putting the pieces back together so that life can makes sense.

- Know that you can still have healthy relationships
  - It is ok to want to be alone
- Create self care practices and release techniques that serve you and support you
  - Find someone you can confide in
  - The abuse does not define who you are, you do
    - You are not worthless
    - You will be okay
    - It will be hard
  - Healing takes time. It is a journey
- Journal if you need to get out some things that you may not be able to say to your abuser
  - Seek professional help or a support group
- Cry, it cleanses your soul, heart, wounds and relieves toxins that may cause your emotional stress
  - Feel it out
- You don't have to deal with every aspect of the abuse and its effects at once, take your time and peel back the layers slowly
  - Enjoy life, it isn't over
  - Evaluate your beliefs and values
- Abuse changes you . It does not change your purpose but may alter how you get there

- You are only responsible and accountable for your change
- You have the right to want better
- You are not wrong for leaving, reporting, speaking out against abuse or standing up for yourself
- Learn to trust yourself
- Breathe
- Do what you love
- Use this experience of abuse to come up with a list of non-negotiable things that you will not accept from anyone no matter what, no exceptions
- You don't have to work on forgiving anyone right now
- Everything is a learning experience even if it feels like a waste of time
- Distance yourself from whoever or whatever doesn't serve you or doesn't make you feel safe
- Regardless of how you made it, you survived, and you will thrive. Give yourself credit.
- You may feel overwhelmed from the departure
- Depending on who the person was that abused you, you may miss them, or regret leaving them
- Abuse is not punishment from God.
- You didn't deserve any abuse.
- Speak over yourself. Build yourself back up
- You are not broken or damaged.

Victorious Proclamations

Affirmations to remind you of the greatness in you that was never lost but (re)discovered to (re)live. Don't just speak them, believe it and become what you speak. Put in the work to bring it all into fruition. Step into your new chapter.

- I have a fundamental right to a nurturing environment.
- I seek peace and no longer tolerate any type of abuse.
- I have the right to be treated with respect.
- I choose who I allow in my space and life.
- I teach others how to treat me based on what I allow.
- I find the lessons and blessings in everything.
- I will not allow life's unfortunate circumstances to define me.
- It is ok for me to be scared, angry, ashamed, or sad. I embrace my feelings and work through them as needed.
- I deserve happiness and will create and enjoy happy moments.
- I will not assume responsibility or accept blame for any abusive behavior. I do not have to carry the load of or for my abuser.
- I hold my abuser accountable for what they did but I hold myself accountable for my healing.
- I trust and forgive myself.
- I believe in who I am and who I am becoming.
- Seeking the approval from others is not essential to my well-being.
- I unapologetically care for myself and my needs.

- I strive for excellence not perfection.
- I am powerful, creative, confident, and assertive.
- I decide how to handle my abuser. My safety and state of mind come first.
- I know God will use everything for my greater good.
- My voice deserves to be heard and presence deserves to be felt.
- I am strong when I am vulnerable and feeling.
- There is life after this.
- I am not broken or damaged.
- I love, cherish, and appreciate me.
- I strive for a better future in spite of my past.
- I am committed to my health and healing.
- There are good people in this world and I am surrounded by them.
- I have a great and strong support system.
- I trust my intuition.
- My cup spills over.
- I am loved and lovable.
- I have a story to tell but I am not my story, nor my circumstances.
- I honor myself, my boundaries, my life, my well-being.

Directory

National Domestic Violence Hotline

1-800-799-SAFE(7233)
1-800-787-3224 (TDD)

National Sexual Abuse Hotline:

1-800-656-4673

Fostering Hearts, www.fostering-hearts.com

MACOSH Healing Network, www.macosh.org

My Help, My Hope, www.myhelpmyhope.org

Sisters Acquiring Financial Empowerment,

www.newsafestart.org

Transition 123, www.transition123inc.org

Women in Distress, www.womenindistress.org

**Connect with organizations, therapists, support groups
in your local area.
Help is there and near for you.
It may not seem like it but you are not alone.**

Thank you for reading our book.

If you enjoyed it, won't you please take a moment to leave a review at your favorite retailer?

ALTMA authors and contributors appreciate you!

Acknowledgments

I HONOR the Creator, who dwells within me, for opening my heart to the power of forgiveness.

I ACKNOWLEDGE the little one inside, who would not be still, until I, the grown-up adult, paid attention to her and met her needs. Then, she could be a child and stop running my grown-up adult life. I AM GRATEFUL to my personal villagers:

•Family---whose love and care have always sustained me.

•Sisterfriends---especially, E Chemeen Johnson, Deborah Randolph-Price, Michaele White-Risbrook, Hortense Hinton-Jackson, Kim Manson, Roz Rhett Webb, Nzingha Sweeney-Sheppard and Karen Walston, for their insights, support, encouragement and feedback as I wrote this manuscript.

•Peter L. Bibby for sharing his masculine energy, which compelled me to go deeper and deeper until Truth was revealed.

•Cher Bartlett, my alternative healthcare practitioner, who uses her gifts to assist me in keeping my body, mind and spirit in alignment, to maintain optimum health.

•C Ann Taylor, psychotherapist extraordinaire, whose expertise has guided me back TO myself, while moving/pushing/dragging me forward to BE myself!

- A special thank you to my friend/proofreader/editor, whose expertise was invaluable.

I THANK Sharisa Robertson for pursuing your vision and

providing myself and other writers with this unique opportunity to share our stories.

I AM GRATEFUL to be of service, through this writing, to all who will read this manuscript.

I ENCOURAGE you to take your own Journey Within.

I AM there on the path.....

And So It Is.

Furelise Smith

****

I would be remiss not to thank The Most High for giving me the wisdom to finally begin to understand "the why's." I acknowledge that I could be in a TOTALLY different place in my journey but I am here, and I am thankful. To my husband Quentin and daughters, Arianna and Jaezlin I love and absolutely adore all 3 of you. I learn from you and through you. You all are the best! To my friends and family, I appreciate you for all the prayers, the love and all of the listening ears you have given.

With love,

Christina "Chris" Jiles

******

I would like to thank God for keeping me in the midst of my storm. He placed people in my path that would not only speak life to me, but would also encourage me and pray for me. I would like to thank my son, Devin Thomas, who provided me with wisdom beyond his years during the lowest periods in my life. Thank you for allowing God to use you. I will forever love you and be grateful to God for blessing me with such an amazing seed. To my Pastor Bishop Walter

Scott Thomas and The New Psalmist Baptist Church family, you were truly my saving grace. When I felt that I was not worthy of God's love, you provided me with the spiritual guidance and nourishment that I needed to grow forward in Christ. You helped me see that my life and my path were covered by God. Bishop Thomas, every sermon that you preach gave me a new hope and I am so grateful for your obedience to God's direction because that gave me strength beyond what I could have ever imagined. Finally, to my mother, Hazel Pittman, who provided me with a place of shelter when I felt I had no place to find refuge. Your actions helped me see that there was hope beyond what I was experiencing. There are so many friends and other family members that stood by me and with me without judgment. To you all I would like to say thank you. I will not list them, as I may leave out someone, but you know who you are and please know that I appreciate you all dearly.

Teresa Mack

******

I would like to acknowledge my good friend Kitara Bingham, when you said yes to living your dream of being an author you gave me the courage to do the same. I would like to thank my mom Vernay and my Aunt Tee, who taught me that you don't always ask permission, sometimes you just do it until someone else tells you no. To my Minende Sisterhood; we have been together seventeen years and counting, thank you for being on this life journey with me. To Master Coach Aprille Franks-Hunt, The Coach Speak & Serve Tribe, LaTara V. Bussey, Precious Foster, and Eboni L. Truss thanks you for helping me see the business woman inside of me who is emerging into her vision. To my son Cornelius you are my greatest joy. To my other family, Minende Sister

Circle and friends thank you so much for your love and support.

E. Chemeen

****

I give all Glory and Praise to God for the opportunity to be a part of such a wonderful collaboration. It's an honor. Thank you so much Sharisa Robertson for the opportunity that you have allowed myself and others in being a part of your Vision that God has given you. To my ROCK, my mom, I am grateful and appreciative of her tenacity. She is a survivor of domestic violence and she has been victorious through the hurt and obstacles that she endured being a battered wife and then a single mom. She has instilled in me the importance of having a relationship with God, and in the ways to acknowledge God so He will direct my path. Thank you mom for teaching me to be a strong Woman of God. My mom believes it's better to trust in God than put confidence in man. THANK YOU MOM!

Expressions and Love to my Kingdom Leaders Apostle Royal & Kimberly McClinton, and special salute to Pastor Kevin Lloyd, my best friend, my king, my covering, my wonderful husband Thank you hubby bear for your unconditional love and support.

Lisa R. Lloyd

****

I am so thankful for this project and honored God chose me for this. I thank my editor, Tamykah, book cover designer, Angela, book promotion coach, LaShaunda. I appreciate from the bottom of my heart, all of the authors in this project, Furelise, Miss Buttafly, E. Chemeen, Cathy, Teresa, Lisa, and Christina. Thank you ladies for trusting me with your stories. Thank you for your patience in bringing this book into manifestation. Appreciation to the writers of the Foreword and Afterword, Kalyn and Thema for your added wisdom and encouragement. Thank you to my loved ones and supporters. My heart is full.

Sharisa T. Robertson

****

My family is my rock. My mother, Joan, and my children, DeVon, Dorian, and Dominique are the source of my inspiration and they have been my healing refuge. I cannot imagine my life or my work without them. They love me unconditionally, and I them. I also have a few very close friends who have been critical to my healing process. I love you all tremendously. And finally, I wish to acknowledge myself. I have been brave and will continue to be so. I honor my past, but I don't live there anymore. This letter was my goodbye to these words and the stories attached to them. I speak life!

Oh! I can't forget the visionary behind this project, Ms. Sharisa Robertson. Your passion for creating healing spaces through literature is to be admired. Thank you for allowing me to be a part of this impactful project.

-Miss Buttafly

****

Bonus Section for Readers

✳

Add Your Letter

Use the bonus section to add your letter to this book as an unofficial author, to your abuser regardless of who or what that is to you. Begin your chapter of having a release and having a voice. There isn't a right or wrong way. Write however you feel. It is OK to be angry, to be scared, even ashamed, but it is even better to get those feelings out of you, especially if you have been holding on to them in for a long time. Pretend you are in the room with your abuser and you have a chance to say anything, and finally everything, you have wanted to say without any interruptions. What would you say? Write it!

Note: This is just for you, and although you can/could also share it with your abuser to have dialogue about what you wrote and your feelings, it is advised to use your discretion. This is for you and your eyes and heart only.

Don't forget to come up with a unique closing signature too.

Here are a few base questions to get you started. Add to or take away as you feel and need to:
- Who abused you?
- What type of abuse did you experience?
- Tell your abuser how their behavior affected you, made you feel.
- What do you want from the abuser, if anything at all?
- What memories stick out the most from being

abused? What has been done and said to you?

- What do you want to get off of your chest and say to, or ask, your abuser?
- What do you wish you could or would have done?
- How will you move forth from this starting today? How will you turn this into a positive for yourself?
- What do you affirm?

Use the blank page to name your chapter!!!

Made in the USA
Columbia, SC
23 December 2019

85679041R00080